✳ persuasive writing

how to make words work for you

CREATIVE BUSINESS SOLUTIONS

*persuasive writing
how to make words work for you nick souter

artwork by   guy billout

STERLING

New York / London
www.sterlingpublishing.com

STERLING and the distinctive Sterling logo are
registered trademarks of Sterling Publishing Co., Inc.

**Library of Congress Cataloging-in-Publication
Data Available**

10 9 8 7 6 5 4 3 2 1

Published by Sterling Publishing Co., Inc.
387 Park Avenue South, New York, NY 10016
© 2007 The Ilex Press Limited
Artwork © Guy Billout
Distributed in Canada by Sterling Publishing
c/o Canadian Manda Group, 165 Dufferin Street
Toronto, Ontario, Canada M6K 3H6

Printed in China
Sterling ISBN-13: 978-1-4027-4836-3
         ISBN-10: 1-4027-4836-1

For information about custom editions, special sales,
premium and corporate purchases, please contact
Sterling Special Sales Department at 800-805-5489
or specialsales@sterlingpub.com.

CD-ROM Contents

There are four interactive software tools on the
attached CD-ROM.

They are:

1. **The Drafting Tool**. This word processor
   will force you to keep writing without
   looking back.
2. **The 5 Whys**. This process will ensure you
   talk about benefits and not merely features.
3. **The Information Map**. This software will
   organize your thoughts into themes that
   support your purpose.
4. **The Organizational Diamond**. This system
   imposes a structure that will make your
   writing more persuasive.

contents

1. How to use this book

From the résumé you type to get your first job interview to the retirement letter you compose at the end of a long career, your ability to write will play a critical role in whether or not you are going to succeed.

Through the written word you'll share your knowledge and understanding, sell your ideas, and persuade people to follow your lead. (That's if you want to be a leader and not a follower.) And you'll need to do that in many different media—letters, emails, faxes, reports, minutes, handwritten notes, press releases, stickies, memos, newsletters, you name it. (One of the most helpful messages I've received was scribbled on a napkin and passed to me under the table during lunch!)

As you will always be short of time, you'll need to write quickly as well as clearly, concisely, accurately, persuasively, and in a manner that engages and holds the attention of your readers. Remember, they don't have much time either.

That's a lot of balls to keep in the air.

And the trouble is, many of us don't like writing. Some of us hate it. We may speak well and know what we want to say, but the glare of an empty page can induce a paralyzing anxiety.

Many writers, even people who make their living by writing, suffer these agonies and crises of confidence. Novelists fear writer's block the way athletes fear injury. But fortunately there is a big difference between fictional writing and good business writing. A novelist conjures something out of nothing. He or she travels to an imaginary world and hopes to come back with a story the rest of us want to read.

That's not what we are going to be doing.

The sort of writing we use in business doesn't require such a hazardous journey. You can stay right where you are and use what you already know. And if there is something you don't know but need to know, you'll be more likely to find it through careful research than through the vagaries of your imagination. Business writing is about purpose and planning, about structure and organization— it's not about art and inspiration.

So, as a business writer, you can dispense with the unreliable services of a muse. (Good riddance!) Instead, you can rely entirely on process.

This book is all about process.

Persuasive writing is a craft. And like all crafts, there is a process that enables you to learn and master it.

We'll do this in six steps:

1. Preparation
2. Planning
3. Drafting
4. Reviewing
5. Rewriting
6. Polishing

Preparation and Planning sound similar but they focus on different things. The section on Preparation is about how we prepare our minds and organize our thoughts and approach. In the section on Planning we look at how to prepare our material and organize our information.

There's some theory in the chapters on Preparation. We'll use a Communication Model to explore the relationship between you and your readers. That will help you choose the medium, style, and tone of voice that best conveys your point of view. And we'll learn how to identify and remove some of the barriers and prejudices that might prevent your message from being clearly understood.

Once you have absorbed the process and theory of mental preparation, it becomes quick, easy, and intuitive. Planning takes longer and is probably the most important phase of the whole communication process. As the saying goes,

"If you fail to plan, you are planning to fail."

We'll start with the single most important element of business communication—your Purpose. Until you know exactly what you want to achieve, you should do nothing. Don't write a word. You can't expect your readers to respond in the way you would like if you haven't decided exactly what it is you want them to do.

Everything you write in business will be intended to inspire change. You will want your readers to either think or act differently after they have absorbed what you have to say. The word "communication" derives from the Latin words *communicare*, meaning "to share," and *communis*, meaning "common." Communication is about sharing a new agreement and understanding.

That can only happen if you have clearly established your desired outcome and structured your message to support it.

Purpose is the DNA that will ensure your words evolve into a piece of persuasive writing.

As soon as you know your purpose, you can decide how to use your time. It doesn't matter if you have a lot or a little, time needs to be divided between the different phases of the writing process. If you are under pressure, then you need to condense the phases and not eliminate one phase altogether. A lot of poor business writing occurs when pressure forces us to start writing before we start thinking. You will get a better communication if you think more and write less. So we'll look at a timeline that can be applied to any writing task, irrespective of how long you have allowed for it.

For many people, the hardest part of writing is getting started. If that is your problem, then you are most likely suffering from nerves and a lack of planning. You need to organize your material.

Information is the raw material of communication.

Sometimes you'll find you have more information than you need, sometimes not enough.

In Section 2, Planning, we'll practice the use of mind mapping to collect, select, and organize information, and then review ten standard formats for structuring it. All of them are useful for different tasks and applications, but we're going to concentrate on one in particular—the Organizational Diamond. This format has been designed specifically to make your writing more persuasive.

Only when Preparation and Planning are complete—when you understand your readers, your purpose, your material, structure, style, and tone of voice—only then will you be ready to write.

Section 3 is Drafting. This is where you first put your thoughts on the page. Surprisingly, it's one of the shortest sections in the entire writing process. It's also one of the easiest, even if you don't enjoy writing.

When drafting, you take the thoughts you organized in the Planning phase and just let them spill out. You write quickly and without stopping. And you don't worry or hold back. You put a gag on your inner critic and just keep going without any concern for spelling, grammar, or punctuation—none of that matters.

Most people, especially perfectionists, find it liberating to write without caring.

And you'll also be surprised by the quality of the words you produce. When you review it at the next stage, you'll discover that the hard work was actually done when you were planning. Suddenly the writing is not so difficult. It may be full of technical errors, but they are easy to fix.

In Section 4, Reviewing, you'll change your perspective. You'll take a break from being the writer and go over the first draft with the critical eye of your reader. Reviewing is all about content and structure. When you are satisfied that you have put the right things in the right place, you can move onto the next stage of the process.

Section 5 is Rewriting. Again, this phase is focused on content. You'll look at making the opening more engaging and the ending more inspiring. You'll add proof to any claims that you are making and ensure that you are never vague, always specific. We'll also look at how you can use Robert Cialdini's Six Weapons of Influence to make your message more persuasive, and we'll consider how best to use any visual information and support. By the end of this stage you will have completed a second draft.

Think of this draft as a working prototype. It does the job. Under pressure, you could probably put it in an envelope or hit "Send." But you'll learn to resist that temptation.

In Section 6 you'll practice the art of Polishing. If you believe that "the devil is in the detail," then you'll understand how important this part of the process is going to be. We'll look at how you can adjust the style and language of your document to make it concise, clear, and correct. Polishing removes all the rough edges from your writing. Your words will flow smoothly and be easier to read. Your writing will become more powerful and create greater empathy with your reader.

The art of good business writing is to make your words replace your reader's thoughts. Polishing is how we make that happen.

By now you may be thinking, "I don't have time for such an involved process." The opposite is true. Most people waste their time by writing without the necessary planning and preparation. As a result, they write hesitantly and slowly with constant revisions and then revisions of revisions. The process is tedious, repetitive, and the final result is nowhere near as good as it could be.

To make matters worse, in all likelihood, the communication will not entirely succeed. A second correspondence will probably be required and more time will be wasted.

The best way to save time is to get it right first time. But that doesn't mean first draft.

The six-stage process will actually streamline your writing. In the workshops we conduct, we find people get to a better result in half the time. That's not because they write faster. It's because their thinking is more focused, they spend less time chewing the end of their pen and wondering what to write next or having to start again. This book works as both a manual and a reference guide.

Chapters 2–11 are the manual that teaches the six-step process. You need to work through these in the order in which they appear. Once you've done that, you can use the Contents page to return to any individual section that you may want to study further.

The exercises at the end of each chapter will help you make the process part of your everyday writing style. Once you have mastered these simple skills, you'll develop a confidence in your ability to write effectively. If you are a perfectionist, you'll stop agonizing and go with the flow. If you are a procrastinator, you'll stop delaying and get on with the job. Whichever you are, you'll find the prospect less daunting.

2. The communication process

Before we start planning, it's worth giving some consideration to the differences between written and verbal communication.

People often say that "talk is cheap." And it's true that when you express your ideas and intentions through speech, there is a sense that you are allowed to revise them later.

The spoken word has a subtle impermanence.

We're never held 100% accountable for the things we say unless we are talking under oath.

An interesting example of this comes from an American company, for whom I used to do a lot of work.

These words always appeared at the top of their standard inter-office memo: "Do not give or take oral instructions and commands."

The written word, on the other hand, brings the promise of commitment.

When we "put it in writing," we are giving an assurance. The implication is, "You can depend on what I'm saying. I've considered it carefully, and I won't change my mind." In the case of a letter, we increase that commitment by signing our name to it. In some instances, this creates a legally binding document.

This commitment is reinforced by the fact that the written word doesn't just disappear. Your speech may vanish into thin air (unless you are being recorded), but your words on a page will exist until they are lost or someone decides to destroy them. And there are cases where it would be illegal to do that.

It's always possible to repeat something that someone has said, but your audience may wonder if you have changed the meaning and added a personal bias. Reported speech can quickly bend the message out of shape and, in extreme cases, create an entirely new and false communication.

But if you show something that has been written, there is no question of bias. The words on the page remain as permanent evidence of the writer's original intent. Those words can then be copied and distributed without distortion. (In this age of email, a written communication can be distributed around the globe in a matter of seconds.)

As well as the outcome, the actual process of communication is very different between talking and writing.

When we talk to someone face to face, only 7% of our communication is conveyed by the words we choose. An additional 38% is transmitted by the tone of our voice. Put the two together and you still don't account for half of what your audience is receiving. A massive 55% comes from your appearance, facial expression, and body language, much of which is unconscious and beyond your control.

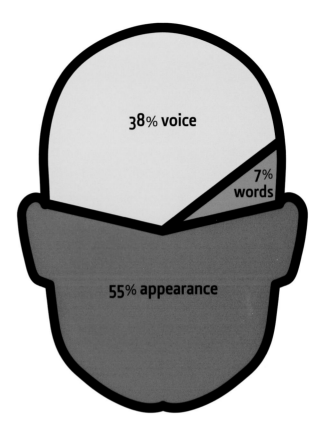

38% voice

7% words

55% appearance

The reverse is true of writing. When you write to someone they will only have your words to interpret. They will have to extract 100% of the meaning from what would be only 7% of the communication in a face-to-face conversation. Your choice of words will have to compensate for the absence of your body, face, and voice.

The message is clear.

When you put your thoughts in writing, your words are going to have to work a lot harder.

There is a medium that sits between the two. The telephone. On the phone you can choose your words and still use your voice to good effect. I've heard it said of a friend that he, "gives good phone." It's a corny expression that makes a good point. He has obviously learned to use the tone, pitch, and speed of his voice to compensate for the loss of 55% of his communication potential.

Telemarketers have learned this lesson very well. In some companies, the operators sit in front of mirrors and look at themselves while they are talking to you. This helps them maintain a constant smile in the hope that their facial expression is subtly captured and transmitted by their voice. In so doing, they can perhaps access a little of that missing 55%.

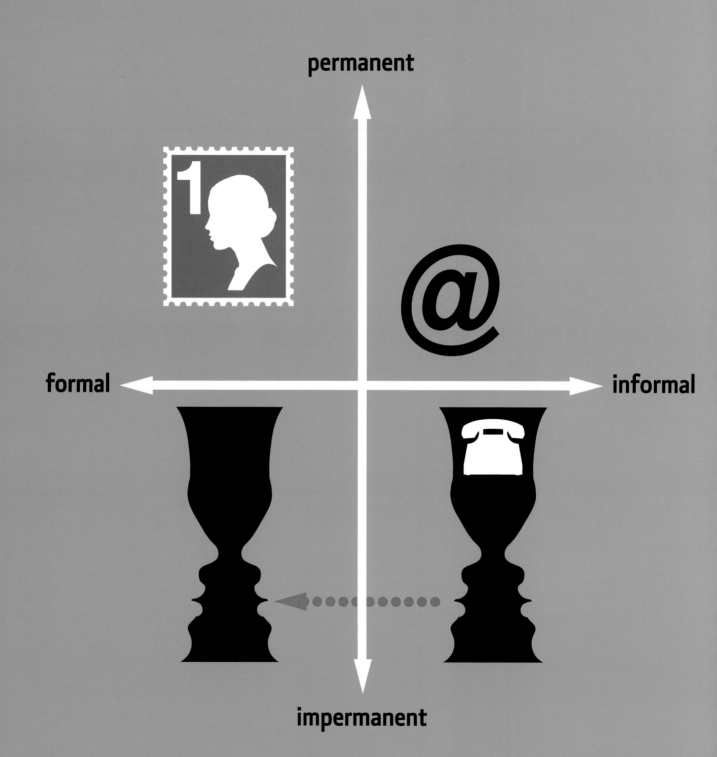

The figure opposite is a matrix that compares the three media. As a general rule one could say that writing is more formal, more committed to its message, less susceptible to misrepresentation, and more public in that it can be copied and circulated—unless marked "Private and Confidential." The spoken word, either by phone or face-to-face, can be less formal, more intimate and personal, easily distorted by repetition, but more private unless recorded. (It's worth remembering that you can't record someone's speech without their permission.)

Once you know someone, you can picture him or her clearly during a conversation in any medium. But the differences between one medium and another can seem exaggerated if you are communicating with someone for the first time.

It's hard to "meet" people over the phone. How often have you had a first encounter over the telephone only to meet the other party in the flesh later, and find that they bear no resemblance to the character you had imagined?

It's the same with the written word. When you receive a letter or email from someone you have never met, you will focus not only on the meaning of the words but also on any clues they contain about the person who sent them. And it's not easy. Sometimes, you'll have to look to the signature to identify even the gender of your correspondent.

This lack of obvious information about the writer implies two things:

● There is potential for misinterpretation leading to miscommunication.
● Your words must work overtime to compensate for you not being there.

And there is one critical difference between writing and speaking.

The written word is not a dialog. It doesn't offer interaction and the opportunity to modify your words as you judge the reaction of your audience.

With the written word, you have to get it right first time.

So let's look at the communication process and identify the barriers you'll need to remove to ensure your thoughts reach your reader and are clearly understood and interpreted in the way you would like.

The illustration opposite shows two Communication Models. We'll look at the left side first. As all communication is two-way, it depicts a writer and a reader. When a reply is sent, the roles then reverse.

In good communication, the writer puts words on the page and they reach the reader without any distortion. The message is absorbed exactly as the writer intended. However, that is rarely the case.

Every reader receives information through a lens-like filter.

What you put on the page might look slightly different when seen through the eyes of the person with whom you are corresponding.

To ensure clear communication, we need to understand the nature of the filter that is distorting the meaning of your words.

The Communication Model on the right side is a diagram of what happens.

These filters, or lenses, are created by the life experience and accumulated prejudices of the person reading your message. They distort everything he or she sees. The problem is, the reader is usually unaware of the distortion these filters are creating.

Let's look at a simple example. Imagine you work for a company that installs central heating and air conditioning and you are sending letters to people on a mailing list you have purchased. You have had no previous contact with these potential customers. Your intention is to offer them a special reduction in the month of January.

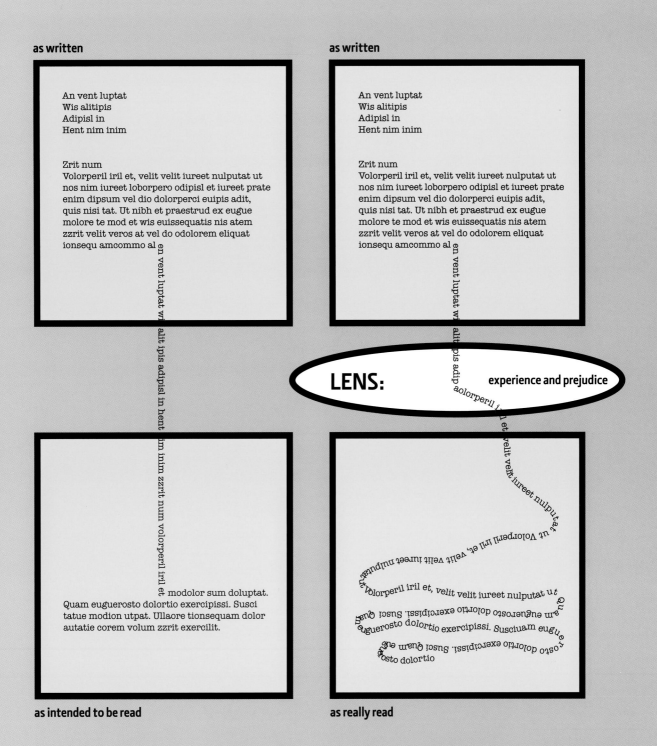

as written

An vent luptat
Wis alitipis
Adipisl in
Hent nim inim

Zrit num
Volorperil iril et, velit velit iureet nulputat ut
nos nim iureet loborpero odipisl et iureet prate
enim dipsum vel dio dolorperci euipis adit,
quis nisi tat. Ut nibh et praestrud ex eugue
molore te mod et wis euissequatis nis atem
zzrit velit veros at vel do odolorem eliquat
ionsequ amcommo al

as written

An vent luptat
Wis alitipis
Adipisl in
Hent nim inim

Zrit num
Volorperil iril et, velit velit iureet nulputat ut
nos nim iureet loborpero odipisl et iureet prate
enim dipsum vel dio dolorperci euipis adit,
quis nisi tat. Ut nibh et praestrud ex eugue
molore te mod et wis euissequatis nis atem
zzrit velit veros at vel do odolorem eliquat
ionsequ amcommo al

LENS: experience and prejudice

en vent luptat wis alitipis adipisl in hent nim inim zzrit num volorperil iril et modolor sum doluptat.
Quam euguerosto dolortio exercipissi. Susci
tatue modion utpat. Ullaore tionsequam dolor
autatie corem volum zzrit exercilit.

ut Volorperil iril et, velit velit iureet nulputat
Volorperil iril et, velit velit iureet nulputat ut
Quam euguerosto dolortio exercipissi. Susci
euguerosto dolortio exercipissi. Suscium eugue
rosto dolortio exercipissi. Susci Quam eugue
rosto dolortio

as intended to be read

as really read

Here's the sort of letter you might write:

FREEZE AND BURN HEATING AND COOLING SYSTEMS
Unheard-of Industrial Estate
Other Side of Town

Dear Mr. Smith,

As summer temperatures soar year on year, and with more hot weather on its way, this is probably a good time to give some consideration to air conditioning.

F&B Heating and Cooling Systems are renowned experts in this field and are currently working in your neighborhood. Because we have many clients not far from your own home, we are in a position to offer you a sizable discount on any installation you may order from us during the month of January.

In the next week, one of our representatives will call on you to discuss whether we can be of service.

You'll find we have a reputation for fast and efficient work, and that our expert engineers have exacting standards of craftsmanship.

If, however, you do not require any work at the moment but know of friends or neighbors who might be interested, please fill out the enclosed prepaid postcard and we will contact them directly without troubling you any further.

Sincerely,

John Brown
Sales Manager

This is not a bad letter. If you were to send it to someone who needs air conditioning and has heard good things about your company, you might meet with a favorable response. But what if it ends up in front of someone who has had bad experiences with people in your field, if not with your company, and who has an innate distrust of salespeople and sales language?

Your message could end up looking like this:

FREEZE AND BURN HEATING AND COOLING SYSTEMS

Unheard-of Industrial Estate
Other Side of Town

Dear Mr. Smith,

As summer temperatures soar year on year, and with more hot weather on its way, this is probably a good time to give some consideration to air conditioning.

(Here we go, here comes the sales pitch.)

F&B Heating and Cooling Systems are renowned experts **(Really! Then how come I've never heard of you?)** in this field and are currently working in your neighborhood. Because we have many clients not far from your own home, we are in a position to offer you a sizable discount on any installation you may order from us during the month of January. **(Ah yes, January being your worst month because everyone has spent their money over the holiday period.)**

In the next week, one of our representatives will call on you to discuss whether we can be of service.

You'll find we have a reputation for fast and efficient work and that our expert engineers have exacting standards of craftsmanship. **(This guy sounds as if he's been reading the garbage in his own brochure.)**

If, however, you do not require any work at the moment but know of friends or neighbors who might be interested, please fill out the enclosed pre-paid postcard and we will contact them directly without troubling you any further. **(Ah! That's how they got my name. I wonder who suggested me?)**

Sincerely,

John Brown
Sales Manager

The message you sent is no longer the one that is being read. Mr. Smith has accumulated prejudices that blind him to the honesty of your pitch.

Prejudice is very subtle. It's rather like a lens in a pair of glasses. We look through it and forget that it's there.

To take this argument one step further, we could say that human beings have a tendency to see what they want to see. The scientist George Stratton conducted an interesting experiment in the 1890s. For eight days he wore a pair of spectacles that inverted the images in his eyes—the world appeared upside-down to him. But after four days, while still wearing these lenses, he found that the world appeared the right way up again. He could walk around his house unaware that a lens was turning his vision on its head.

The fact that these lenses of prejudice become unnoticed leads us to a simple conclusion. It is this:

If the reader is not going to allow for prejudice and distortion, the writer must.

We need to understand and predict how the reader is going to react to two elements of your communication.

The content of your message
The style of your writing

Only when we have considered them both can we draft a letter that passes through the reader's lenses without being bent out of shape.

Summary and Action points

1. The written word is fundamentally different from the spoken word.

- The written word promises commitment, lasts until it is lost or destroyed, is less susceptible to distortion, can be reproduced and distributed, can be legally binding, but can be less personal and intimate.

- The spoken word is less binding, can easily be distorted by memory or reported speech, but is more interactive, and is more personal and intimate.

2. When people read your words, their filters of experience and prejudice can distort your intended meaning.

3. To communicate clearly, you need to understand and anticipate your readers' reaction to both the style and content of your writing.

Exercise

Find a piece of correspondence you have received recently and try to identify the lenses and filters through which you first read it.

3. Understanding your reader

You need to know four things about your readers before you can bypass their filters and lenses. I call them the "4 Ps." They are:

- **Personality**
- **Prejudice**
- **Pressures**
- **Position**

Their Personality will dictate how they like to give and receive information—their communication style.

Their Prejudice is created by their experience, beliefs, and attitudes—some of which we may know or can discover.

The Pressure exerted on them will come from the context of your communication—what's happening to them at the time they receive it. And further pressure will come from the culture in which they are working—the expectations of their company and of their colleagues.

Lastly, their Position is where they stand relative to the changes you would like them to make in either their thoughts or their actions.

Let's look at all four in some detail.

Personality

We're all different. We pride ourselves on it, and some of us wear our individuality like a badge of honor. It's a competitive asset. To quote management analyst Peter Drucker: "The individual is the central, rarest, most precious capital resource of our society."

We are encouraged to revel in this individuality. According to Eleanor Roosevelt: "Remember always that you not only have the right to be an individual, you have an obligation to be one."

However, this has serious implications for how we communicate.

Human beings like to receive information in much the same way they like to give it.

Our individuality would suggest we are all on different wavelengths—we're all transmitting but not receiving. So how do we get through to one another?

Fortunately, we're not quite as different as we might like to think. Broadly speaking, we can all be placed in one of four easy-to-recognize categories. This makes understanding each other's communication preferences a great deal easier. And it gives us a better chance of tailoring our words so that they are appropriate to our reader.

To do this we're going to use a profiling system called HBDI—the Herrmann Brain Dominance Instrument. If this sounds torturous, it's not. HBDI is one of the simplest and most intuitive profiling tools within the world of Human Resources.

If you have ever worked for a large corporation, or even been for an interview at one, you have probably come across Myers Briggs, DISC, Personalysis, or Emergenetics. They are all intended to do much the same thing. They investigate personal preferences so that we can build a simple profile that then enables us to predict how someone is likely to act under certain circumstances. It also tells us how they like to communicate.

This science dates back to the psychologist Carl Jung who made the observation that human beings can be divided into two groups—introverts and extroverts. Jung's work was developed further by the team of Myers and Briggs who created a matrix of 16 personality types.

Their observations are startlingly accurate. But 16 is too big a number for us to work with here. We need something simpler.

A compatible system was developed by educational psychologist Ned Herrmann. He looked at the two most prominent theories and realized he could combine them to create a simple model that can promote better teamwork and communication. A brief history of his concept makes it easier to understand and use.

During the 1950s, Dr. Roger Sperry, a psycho-biologist working in California, introduced a theory that has gained wide acceptance—the notion of a left brain and a right brain.

Scientists had known for a long time that the human brain is divided into two hemispheres. Sperry's contribution, which won him the Nobel Prize, was to understand the different functions performed in these separate hemispheres.

This illustration shows how he divided the workings of the two halves. According to Sperry, the left brain is predominantly rational, and handles analysis, arithmetic, organization, and language. The right brain concentrates on visualization, spatial relationships, aesthetics, and emotion.

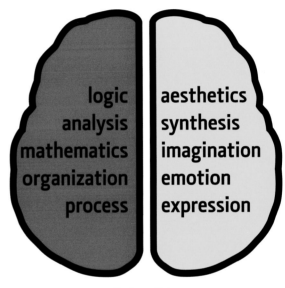

The Sperry Brain

This concept has entered our language and is used idiomatically to describe creative people as "right-brained" and logical people as "left-brained."

He also made the observation that,

whenever we are faced with a choice, we express a preference.

In much the way we prefer to use one hand more than another, or kick a ball with one foot more than the other, we also prefer to use one side of our brain more than the other.

That being the case, we could start our reader analysis by simply asking, "Is this a left-brained or right-brained audience?" In so doing, we'd make some useful observations.

But we can do more than that. Another brain researcher, Paul MacLean, developed an entirely different concept. While chief of the Laboratory of Brain Evolution and Behavior in Maryland, he unveiled his triune—three-in-one—model of the brain. His arrangement was not left and right but top and bottom. Or upper and lower.

MacLean studied the way in which our brain has evolved. About 200 million years ago, human beings emerged into the world with a "reptilian" brain that controlled essential bodily functions and which provided a "fight or flight" mechanism to protect us from predators.

This reptilian brain was situated on top of our spine where it remains to this day. However, 140 million years later, it evolved and added a new compartment. This sub-brain is our limbic system, or mammalian brain, and is built on top of its reptilian ancestor. It brought some interesting new competencies and abilities—most notably, emotion. When humans developed feelings, we abandoned the cold-hearted behavior of our reptilian history and started to care for our young and form communities.

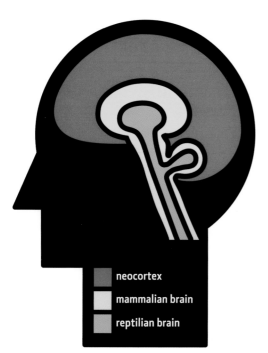

neocortex

mammalian brain

reptilian brain

The MacLean Brain

Evolution didn't stop there. Just a few million years ago, our brains added yet another extension. This extension, once again built on top of the old, now accounts for 80% of our brain mass. It is the neocortex. It houses our intellect and cerebral faculties. It separates us from all other primates by allowing us to think, to communicate in language, to make and enjoy music, and to reflect on the meaning of things.

In common language, when we talk about our "head" we are usually referring to our neocortex. When we talk about our "heart" we are referring to our mammalian brain or limbic system—our feelings.

The diagram on page 28 shows how the three brains are organized. For our purposes, let's ignore the reptilian brain. Its basic functions have little bearing on our understanding of how we communicate.

That leaves us with the mammalian brain or limbic system on the bottom and the neocortex or intellect on the top. The figure on the right looks at their different competencies.

As with Sperry's model, the duality leaves us with a choice and encourages a preference. And it's true, some people tend to trust their intellect more than their feelings and others do the exact opposite.

Once again, we could start our reader analysis by saying, "Does this person trust their thoughts

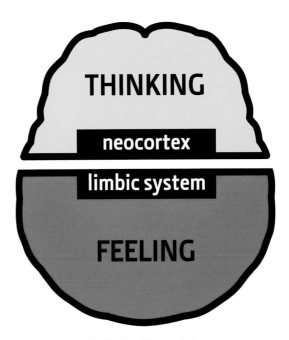

The Two-Part MacLean Brain

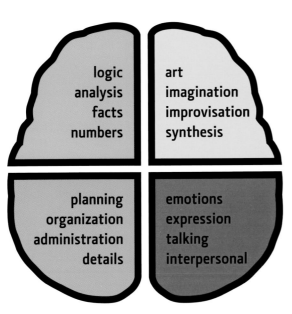

The Herrmann Brain

or trust their feelings? Do they listen to their head or their heart?" We'd make some valuable observations by doing this, and we could use them to guide the way in which we express ourselves.

However, Ned Herrmann studied these apparently different theories and realized that they could be combined into one unified model—one that gives us a very clear insight into how a reader will want to receive your information. He overlaid MacLean's theory with Sperry's to produce the concept you see on the left. He put together the left and right with the upper and lower brains.

There are now four color-coded quadrants. Once you learn how to recognize where your reader belongs, this system becomes very quick and intuitive.

The Blue Quadrant

The upper-left quadrant is a combination of left-brain logic and upper-brain intellect. People who prefer to operate in this quadrant are what we are going to call "Analyzers."
How do you spot one?

> Easy. Blue-Quadrant Analyzers appear unemotional—they are not interested in your feelings, they want the facts. If you are writing a proposal, they will want the recommendation up front, the information to be brief and precise, and your ideas to be supported and substantiated. No waffle. No pie in the sky. Give them the numbers.

They are obsessed with detail and accuracy and will study graphs and charts as carefully as they will your words.

> In opening a communication with them, forget platitudes and niceties. Be respectful, but get to the point. They don't want to write back and answer your questions about their health or family holiday. And they won't. Do you recognize the type?

Before we move onto the next quadrant, list five people you know who would most likely belong among the Blue-Quadrant Analyzers.

The Green Quadrant

The lower-left Green Quadrant combines left-brain logic with the emotions of the lower brain's limbic system. This is where "Organizers" belong.

> The Green Quadrant is all about safekeeping. Organizers are conspicuous because of their love of systems and process. They are innately risk-averse and like to take things one step at a time. They like to be spoon-fed information.

They hate ambiguity and uncertainty. They don't take chances.

> On the upside, the "Greens" always know their stuff. Their active emotions mean they will respect your feelings and appreciate your efforts.

But on the downside, they can appear painfully anal-retentive.

> List five of them you know.

The Yellow Quadrant

The upper right quadrant is where the right brain's imagination meets the intellect of the upper brain's neocortex. People who combine these thinking preferences are "Explorers."

This quadrant is diametrically opposed to the process-focused organizers of the green quadrant, and so it should be no surprise to find that Explorers don't enjoy step-by-step explanations. Instead, they want to see the big picture and then be given a conceptual framework so that they can explore the subject and not be limited by current knowledge and data.

They prefer imagery to facts and figures, and like spontaneity and experimentation. The Yellow quadrant is where creative thinkers tend to live.

Explorers are good at getting things started but bad at getting them done. You'll find them unstructured in written communication, but brimming with ideas and enthusiasm.

Nominate five Yellow Explorers that you know.

The Red Quadrant

The lower-right Red Quadrant is where the right brain's imagination works with the lower brain's emotions. In the language of HBDI, they are "Sensors."

As the layout of the model suggests, Sensors are diametrically opposed to the Blues. While the Blues are worrying about the facts and the numbers, the Reds are all about people and feelings.

They are passionate and will react spontaneously to whatever you write. Their correspondence is like ping-pong. They like it to go back and forth.

They would prefer face-to-face communication, and struggle with too much data, and too many charts and diagrams. Written communication is probably not their strong suit because their emotions run high and it's not always the best medium for them to express their feelings. They are a highly enthusiastic group but, when facts get in the way of human issues, they soon suffer from frustration, and this can lead to anger.

However, the Reds will always be sensitive to your feelings and will want to know about your health and family holiday. So it's a good idea to start your correspondence with a personal touch.

Think of five Red Sensors that you know.

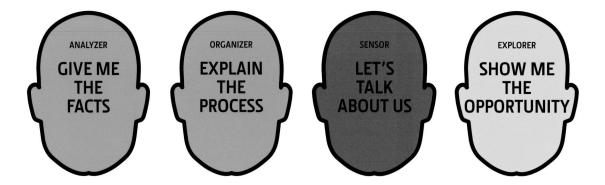

The four colored heads above give you an idea as to how these different personality types want you to communicate with them. Later, we'll look at your personal style and see how it relates to your readers and how you might have to control your natural tendencies when committing words to the page.

Frequently, you'll find yourself writing to a group of people who are a mix of these different profiles.

When that happens, you'll have to structure your correspondence so that it contains something for everyone and particularly for the key decision-makers.

For the moment, let's take a simple example and see how it might have to be rewritten to make it work for each of the four quadrants.

In this instance, you must write to a client to explain that the delivery of his order has been delayed. You are waiting for components to be shipped from China. However, storms and flooding in the area of Wuhan have made the roads impassable. You must inform him of a new delivery date and apologize for the delay.

Blue Quadrant Audience

Dear Mr. Blue,

I regret to inform you that your order, No. 75545, will now be delivered on March 22nd, and apologize for this delay of eight days.

Our parts shipment left Wuhan on the 8th, but was held up by flooding in the region south of the city. However, our haulage company, JTC, have successfully transferred the consignment to China Rail.

It will now be air freighted via Hong Kong (I attach a bill of landing from our Hong Kong office), on Cathay Pacific CX779 and brought to you directly from our depot at the airport.

If you have any questions, please don't hesitate to call me.

Sincerely,

You

Green Quadrant Audience

Dear Mr. Green,

I regret to inform you that your order, No. 75545, will be eight days late in delivery.

I sincerely apologize for this inconvenience and would like to explain the cause of the delay and the measures we have undertaken to ensure the consignment will reach you on March 22nd.

JTC, our haulage company, loaded your parts on March 8th and departed Wuhan the following day. However, severe flooding south of the city meant the roads were impassable and the trucks returned to our depot. Mr. Lee, our dispatch manager, decided to switch the consignment to China Rail, as their service is unaffected by the weather conditions. The crates will reach Macao on the 13th and clear customs there. They will arrive in Hong Kong on the 15th and be air freighted by Cathay Pacific on the 17th.

We anticipate delivery to your office during the afternoon of the 22nd.

If you'd like to track the progress of your shipment, please go to our website and use tracking number 444888.

Any further questions, please don't hesitate to call.

Sincerely,

You

Red Quadrant Audience

Dear John Red,

I sincerely apologize for the delay in the delivery of your machine parts. I appreciate that this places unnecessary pressure on you and your team, and I'd like to assure you that we are doing everything possible to remedy the situation.

As you know, the consignment was to travel by road from Wuhan. Unfortunately, the area south of the city has now been declared a disaster zone with hundreds of families displaced due to flooding. There was no way the trucks could safely make it through, and our drivers made the sensible decision to turn back.

Mr. Lee, our dispatch manager, has worked through the night and moved heaven and earth to get the shipment onto China Rail—they are doing everything they can to help under very trying circumstances. They have given us an assurance that the containers will reach Macao safely, where they can be transferred to Hong Kong for air freighting back here.

We hope to make a delivery to you on the 22nd.

Please feel free to call me anytime if there is anything more I can do to help. I'm at the office or on my cellphone, 073-555-4557.

Best regards,

You

Yellow Quadrant Audience

Dear John Yellow,

I sincerely regret to say that your order has been caught up in the flooding disaster south of Wuhan. (This hasn't attracted much press here, but if you go to www.newsdaily/wuhan/floods you'll see just what a terrible mess the place is in.)

We've looked at a number of transport options to get the consignment to you as quickly as possible—airfreight directly from Wuhan, or train to Macao with a connection to Cathay Pacific out of Hong Kong. (The latter looks most promising and could give us a delivery date of the 22nd.)

Alternatively, we could wait for conditions to improve and go with the original plan. I'd have to get back to you with a revised delivery schedule.

Let's talk, review our alternatives, and decide what you feel would be the best course of action.

Best regards,

You

Comparing the four letters, you can see the emphasis shifts to reflect the fact focus of Mr. Blue, a concern for process with Mr. Green, a need to understand the people issues with Mr. Red, and an exploration of the opportunity with Mr. Yellow.

Prejudice

As we saw in the last chapter, prejudice comes from the accumulation of experience and ideas that form an invisible filter or lens over the eyes of the reader. And while the reader might not be aware of those lenses, the writer can be. And must be.

As part of your preparation process, always ask yourself this very basic question:

"Why might the reader be unsympathetic to my message?"

Let's look at a very simple example. You are writing to your employer because you want to discuss a salary increase. Why might he be unsympathetic?

1. **He isn't aware of the contribution you have personally made.**
2. **He knows your performance is good but it's not long since your last raise.**
3. **He knows the company's profits are down and he can't justify salary reviews.**
4. **He thinks you are great to have around but doesn't rate your work that highly.**
5. **He undervalues your role in the company.**
6. **He knows he can replace you easily for the same money as you are on.**
7. **He only reviews salaries at the end of the year.**
8. **He attributes your success to someone else or to the team as a whole.**
9. **He's too busy to worry about you at the moment.**
10. **He wants his bosses to think he's tough and cost-conscious.**

These ten different reasons require ten radically different letters. If this sounds elementary, it is. But it's surprising how often we overlook the prejudice of our readers because we are seeing the world through our eyes and not theirs.

You may have extremely good and valid reasons for wanting a salary review. But listing them will be ineffectual if you have not considered the prejudices that may render them worthless or irrelevant.

This question only takes a moment to answer but will help you get inside your reader's mind and anticipate some of the barriers you will have to overcome.

Pressures

Irrespective of what your reader may personally feel about what you have to say, he or she will be influenced by pressures that are completely external to your communication.

These pressures can also cause a distortion of your words and meaning. They fall into two groups that we'll call "Culture" and "Context."

Culture

All organizations have not one, but two cultures —a formal one and a hidden one.

The formal culture is usually publicized by the organization. It's a reflection of its brand values. For example, the formal culture of Apple is that it prizes innovation and design above all things. Its slogan is "Think Different." The formal culture of Virgin Atlantic is "Brilliant customer service that's innovative, fun, and value for money." They describe themselves as Consumer Champions. Procter & Gamble want to "provide superior products that improve the lives of the world's consumers." Their culture is built on values of "leadership, integrity, trust, and a passion for winning."

It's easy to detect the formal culture of a company. Just read their literature, their annual report or Google their "name + brand values," as I just did. In less than five minutes I knew the formal cultures and values of Apple, Virgin, and P&G.

If you were writing a letter to any of these companies, it would be sensible for the content and style of your letter to reveal that your point of view is compatible with their own outlook. Unless you are making a complaint and looking for a confrontation, you would want your reader to feel that you shared the values of the company's culture.

However, the hidden culture is another matter altogether. The hidden culture exists behind closed doors. You won't find it on their website or in the CEO's annual newsletter.

The hidden culture is the way things really are.

And sometimes, there's a big difference between the formal and the hidden. When I was in advertising, I worked for a FMCG (Fast-Moving Consumer Goods) brand whose formal culture was that they rewarded innovation and fresh thinking. To keep me out of court, let's say they were called "Bloggo." While devoted to customer satisfaction, they encouraged the belief that the corporation was built on a willingness to try new things. It wanted to be seen at the cutting edge of new product development and marketing initiatives.

The truth, in my experience, was somewhat different. The company's glory days were long gone. While Bloggo had once been progressive and successful, it had retreated to intense risk aversion in leaner times. The hidden culture was what I'd call a fear culture. Most of the management team were more concerned with avoiding the consequences of failure than they were with chasing the fruits of success. As a result, new ideas were routinely discarded in favor of a more conservative approach.

Now let's imagine you are going to write to someone in a senior position at Bloggo. You could toe the corporate line and acknowledge only the formal culture. Your letter could espouse the values of innovation and forward thinking. Trouble is, you'd be completely at odds with the reality of your reader's situation.

On the other hand you could shoot yourself in the foot by openly acknowledging the hidden culture. These cultures are hidden for a reason. The organization does not want to be defined by such negative values. The problem is that these are the values that will act as filters when your reader looks at your correspondence.

You are on a tightrope.

Your letter must be a perfect balance of embracing the virtues of the formal culture while subtly accepting the realities of the hidden one.

Only then can you deliver a message that is not distorted by the prejudices of your reader's working environment.

Context

Culture is not the only force at work. The events of the recent past will also be uppermost in your reader's mind. Before planning your communication, ask this simple question: "What's going on in my reader's life?"

> Consider the personal as well as the professional. For example, let's imagine you are going to write a long and detailed proposal to a client. Your recommendation will be costly, but you have ample evidence to prove that it will generate a good return on investment.

How would your communication be affected by knowing any of the following to be true about the client?

- **Her company has just declared record year-end profits**
- **Her company is in a disastrous slump and receiving bad press**
- **She has just had her third child**
- **She is about to be promoted**

Again, as with cultural forces, radically different correspondence is required in each instance. After a record year, you'd emphasize your opportunity in a mood of exuberant optimism. After a disastrous year, you'd stress that yours is a safe and secure investment. If she's rushed off her feet and sleeping badly, you'd keep it simple and be mindful of her time and attention span. And, if she is to be promoted, you'd want to understand her departmental plans and be sure to engage the support of her successor.

> These crude examples make a very simple point.

Your correspondence can be affected by events that are completely unrelated to it.

Before you start, try to figure out what they might be. And be prepared to allow for them.

Position

If your communication is intended to persuade or influence the reader to think or do something differently (and it often is), then imagine he or she is standing on a seesaw. One end represents total compliance with your recommendation. The other end represents rejection and lack of interest. In the middle is a tipping point.

The process of persuasion is one where you move your reader along the seesaw until they cross that tipping point. This cannot be done in a single leap. It has to be done in steps—one at a time.

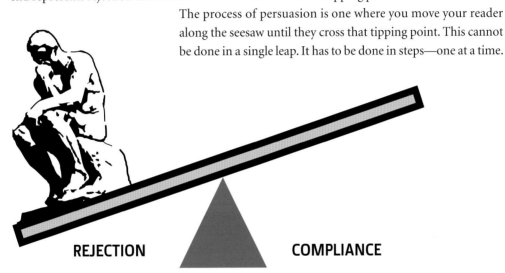

REJECTION   **COMPLIANCE**

The figure below describes the stages of change through which your reader must pass to move from rejection to compliance. This model, developed by psychologists James Prochaska and Charles DiClemente, is called the Transtheoretical Model of Change. They worked in the field of addictive behavior and were particularly interested in persuading people to stop smoking.

They discovered five distinct stages:

1. Pre-contemplation
2. Contemplation
3. Preparation
4. Action
5. Maintenance

PRE-CONTEMPLATION | CONTEMPLATION | PREPARATION | ACTION | MAINTENANCE

Their model applies to any process of persuasion, particularly if resistance is involved.

Imagine I am a young man and that you work for a company that sells life insurance. You write and inform me that you have a policy with particular benefits for a healthy 25-year-old, such as myself. It's a good offer, affordable and sensible. I skim half of it and throw it in the trash.

> Why? It's well-written and of genuine value. Why do I reject it with so little thought? The answer is that I'm on the far left of the seesaw at Stage 1, Pre-contemplation.

This means that I'm not receptive to the offer you are making. I'm not really hearing it. At 25, I'm healthy and think I'll live forever. I don't need you and I'm not interested.

> However, I meet a girl and we decide to marry. Inevitably, there is much talk of our future. And money. We talk about the possibility of children. And money. About houses. And money. Married friends start to tell me the costs of school, clothing, and so on. After a while, I move one step to the right on the seesaw. I'm now in Stage 2, Contemplation. Financial planning is suddenly on my radar. I'm starting to realize that I should put money aside, but I'm not yet doing anything about it. I'll probably procrastinate and put it off and could stay at this stage for some time.

One year later I'm married. The reality of being a sole provider is starting to dawn on me. Were my wife to quit work, we'd need money. Fast. So I move one step to the right again. I'm now in Stage 3, Preparation. In this stage I'll start to make plans and look at a timeline for action. Perhaps I'll decide to start investing after my next pay raise. I'm now in the middle of the seesaw, wobbling between planning and action. Preparation is usually a shorter stage because the timeline is now driving the agenda.

> January comes, I get my annual raise and decide to investigate my options. If you gave up when I failed to respond in Stage 1, I'll have probably forgotten about you. But if you have stayed with me through the process, you'll now reap your reward. The seesaw has tipped and I'm in Stage 4, Action. I invest in one of your financial plans.

After a while, this behavior becomes habitual. I'm now an investor. I'm one of your clients, and as I earn more, I'll probably invest more. I've reached the end of the seesaw and am in Stage 5, Maintenance.

There are two key things to learn from Prochaska and DiClemente's work.

- People only move one stage at a time
- You must know where they are on the seesaw when you first approach them

There's no point in trying to move people farther than they are prepared to go. They will simply disengage. The principle is simple. Determine their position, then move them one stage at a time.

Summary and Action points

1. Consider your reader and remember the 4 Ps: Personality, Prejudice, Pressures, and Position.

2. Identify your reader's profile. Are they:

- A blue-headed analyst only interested in the facts
- A green-headed organizer who wants to know the process
- A red-headed sensor who cares about the people issues
- A yellow-headed explorer who's interested in the creative opportunity

3. Study their communication preferences and identify the key motivators you will need to use.

4. Try to determine the prejudices that may encourage your reader to dismiss your ideas or proposal. Why might they be unsympathetic to your message?

5. Consider the outside Pressures on your reader. They are:

- Culture—both Formal and Hidden
- Context—recent events that might affect or distort the interpretation of your communication

6. When writing with the intent to persuade, consider your reader's position or Stage of Change. Move them one stage at a time.

4. Understanding yourself

A similar "4 Ps" apply to you as the earlier four did to your readers. Before planning any correspondence, you need to be familiar with your own:

- **Personality**
- **Prejudices**
- **Pressures**
- **Performance Style**

Fortunately, it's easier to make the necessary observations because you have all the inside information.

In writing, your Personality will be expressed by your communication style and your writing style. They are subtly different and we need to look at both.

As with your readers, your Prejudices may not be obvious to you, but you must learn to detect those lenses if they are not to distort the meaning of your words.

Pressures come from your context and culture, and may exert a force to which you have become so accustomed that you have ceased to notice it.

And your Performance style depends on whether you are a perfectionist or a procrastinator.

Personality

On paper or on a computer screen, your personality will emerge from what you say and how you say it—content and style.

The two overlap but, for the purpose of this exercise, let's separate them as best we can. We'll say that the content and structure of your message is part of your communication style and your tone of voice and language define your writing style.

Communication Style

Through intuition and observation, you can usually work out the communication preferences of your reader—unless you know nothing about them at all. And even then, the nature of their work and the subject of your correspondence will give you some clues as to how they like to read and write.

However, we can be a little more rigorous and scientific in analyzing your own preferences. And once you know your default settings you'll be able to change them and write in a way that will meet your reader's needs.

The illustration opposite is a questionnaire that will help you do a simple self-profile.

Start with Map 1 and circle the eight elements you most strongly prefer. Don't worry which quadrant they are in. Just choose the ones that really appeal to you. Then move to Map 2 and circle the eight elements you think will be most important over the length of your career.

Finally, move to Map 3 and circle the eight requirements that would be part of your ideal job. Find the roles you'd most like to fulfill.

Now you need to work out your score. Go to Map 4 and, referring back to the choices you made, enter how many circles you put in each quadrant in each of the three diagrams.

The easiest way to do this is quadrant by quadrant. Start with the upper left—the Blue. Count up the number of circles in Maps 1, 2, and 3 and enter them in their respective boxes. Then do the same with Green, Red, and Yellow. When you've finished, add up the totals for each quadrant and enter them into the Total boxes.

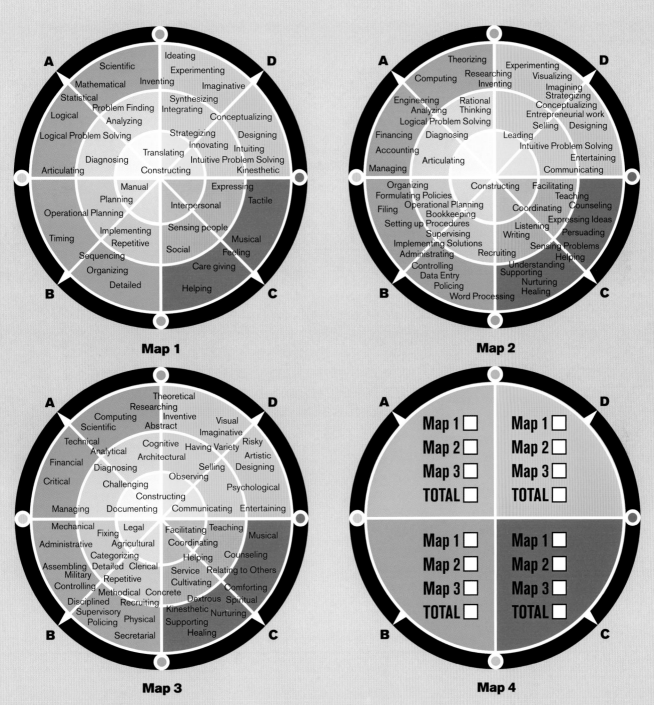

Map 1

Map 2

Map 3

Map 4

Preference Indicator Exercise from *The Whole Brain Business Book* by Ned Herrmann, published by McGraw-Hill, © 1996, reproduced with the permission of The McGraw-Hill Companies.

The quadrant with the highest total number is your dominant quadrant, and represents your preferred style of communication. This is the way you would like to give and receive information. It's possible that you could be double dominant and have an equally high score in two quadrants. If this is the case, consider yourself a combination of the two. It simply means your style is broader.

Look at the four heads shown here and see how their styles clash. It's most obvious when two diametrically opposed quadrants want to communicate. The experimental and creative approach of a Yellow is in stark contrast to the process-driven and highly organized requirements of a Green. Similarly, the touchy-feely human values of a Red are very much at odds with the hard facts and figures that appeal to a Blue.

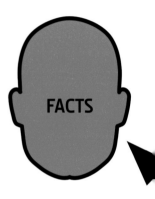

You'll find a greater level of sympathy between quadrants that are on the same side of the vertical division. Reds and Yellows belong in the same right-brain, creative hemisphere, while Blues and Greens come from the left-brain, logical hemisphere. This tends to reduce the level of conflict in their preferred styles. But it doesn't remove it entirely.

And so it is above and below the horizontal division. Blues and Yellows share a preference for the intellectual powers of the neocortex while Greens and Reds are more driven by the emotions of their mammalian brains.

When contemplating a communication, it's necessary to understand how your preferences will relate to your reader's. Once you know that, you can write in a way he or she will find easy to read and which will reduce any unconscious resistance that may be provoked by a clash of styles.

Years ago, I had a client with whom I was always in conflict. Every meeting was an agony of petty disagreements and disappointments. Often, we would reach a successful conclusion but feel exhausted by the process. I put this down to a clash of personalities. But, strangely, we got on like a house on fire outside the office. We shared a sense of humor and enjoyed many of the same things—books and music. In business, we also wanted the same things. There was no real conflict of objectives.

It took me a long time to realize that our clash was fundamentally over our communication styles. He was a strong Green and I was a strong Yellow. He regarded my approach as haphazard and undisciplined. I considered him to be a process maniac and anally retentive. (He was both!)

If I wrote half a page he'd send me back a three-page reply, most of which I only glanced at.

However, he was the client. In any confrontation he was likely to win. If I was going to succeed in selling him my ideas, something had to change.

Over the months we worked together, I learned to recognize his style and adjust mine to meet it. I never had to change my point of view or recommendations. I just changed the way I communicated them to him. He wanted reassurance, and so I gave him process, structure, and detail. And a plan B. Eventually, we built a very good rapport and found ourselves in agreement on most things. And, although I would never have expected it at the outset, we became a good team.

It's easy to confuse a conflict of communication styles with a conflict of interests.

That's why it is so important to align your style with that of your reader. And the only way to do that is to understand both.

Writing Style

As well as a communication style, we all develop a writing style or tone of voice. And often it's very different from the tone of voice we might use when we are talking.

My lawyer sends me emails and letters that sound as if they have been dictated by Adolf Hitler, but, face-to-face, he's a rather sensitive and thoughtful person. He probably feels his writing is businesslike and appropriate to the subject matter. I doubt he has ever wondered if it is appropriate to his recipient.

We need to recognize our own writing style if we are going to control it. If I were to suggest that you write a sample piece now, you'd be self-conscious and produce something that's not truly representative of your natural voice. So go to either your filing cabinet or the "Sent Items" folder on your email server and pull out two or three lengthy pieces you have written in the last couple of months. By "lengthy," I mean a page or more. If you can, copy or print them out so that you can take a close look at them and make some notes. (As this book is about writing for business, don't choose letters to family and friends.)

The measures below will help you assess your style. Read through the material and then go through each of them and give yourself a mark from 1 to 10 (1 on the left, 10 on the right).

FORMAL   **CASUAL** ☐

SERIOUS   **HUMOROUS** ☐

BRIEF   **WORDY** ☐

COOL   **WARM** ☐

STIFF   **RELAXED** ☐

GUARDED   **OPEN** ☐

DISTANT   **CLOSE** ☐

UNEMOTIONAL   **EMPATHIC** ☐

STRUCTURED   **UNSTRUCTURED** ☐

ME FOCUSED   **YOU FOCUSED** ☐

PRECISE   **VAGUE** ☐

TIGHT   **FREE-FLOWING** ☐

Pick your top three scores and see if you can define your writing style. You may find it hard to be objective. When using these measures, there is a tendency for people to give themselves 5s, as that number seems to suggest a norm. And it would appear that most of us, for whatever reason, think we are normal!

The illustration at right gives some suggestions that might inspire you.

A more effective approach is to ask someone else to read your words and define your style. In an instant, they'll be able to see how you come across. Be careful whom you choose, as you might feel insulted. But their opinion will give you a genuinely objective point of view. It's also easier.

The purpose of the exercise is to know the style to which you will default when writing in a hurry or under pressure.

Only when you know your style can you change it and make sure it's appropriate for your subject and your readers.

1
Cool, calm, collected
2
Straight talking
3
Short and Sharp
4
The Protagonist
5
The Schoolteacher
6
The Detail Fanatic
7
The Friendly Advisor
8
The Therapist
9
Mr. Honesty
10
The Wanderer
11
The Enthusiast
12
The Nutty Professor

Prejudices

You, too, are wearing lenses that affect the way you see the world. You may not be aware of them, but your experiences and attitudes are subtly revealed in the way you write. You need to bring these feelings into consciousness so that you can decide if they truly belong in your communication.

> For example, I have long held a deeply felt prejudice against the tax authorities. I've had some altercations with them in the past and, rightly or wrongly, have come to believe that they are uninterested in my personal circumstances and simply want my money—as much of it as they can get.

This prejudice, or lens, has affected the tone of voice in my correspondence with them. Usually, I'm defensive and expecting the worst. And I'm sure it shows. I'm polite and I'm meticulous in making sure my facts are correct. But my tone is always cool and wary, as if poised for confrontation.

Recently, after failing to resolve a disagreement, I decided to call instead of write. Thanks to the tax office's efficient reference numbering system, I was soon talking to the person in charge of my file. She was delightful—helpful, thoughtful, and genuinely motivated to resolve the problem in a way that was fair to me. I was surprised. But then thinking about it, her correspondence to me had been no more than adding numbers to standard tax forms and putting them in an envelope. I'd never even seen her signature.

> Suddenly, the tone, attitude, and style of my letters seemed inappropriate and probably counter-productive.

It's easy to allow the prejudice you feel toward an organization to create a bias in your correspondence with an individual.

> It's important to remember that it's impossible to write to an organization. We can only write to an individual (or collection of individuals). So we need to be mindful of our prejudices and not allow them to make an unconscious appearance in our language and style. Even if we are not aware of them, our readers will be. And it will affect their judgment of what we have to say.

And when writing to someone you do know, you still need to ask the question: "What prejudices and beliefs do I have about this person that may be subtly reflected in this correspondence?"

Don't shy away from the notion that you do have prejudices. The word has some very negative connotations. It suggests bigotry, racism, and unfounded condemnation. But its meaning is simply to pre-judge. It doesn't mean to condemn. And sometimes we pre-judge a person or situation in the most positive way we can. We don't always expect and see the worst.

Nevertheless a prejudice, whether it is positive or negative, must be reviewed in the context of the communication. You might feel overwhelmingly positive about someone to whom you have to write a very critical and damning communication. What do you want them to hear—your positive prejudice or your negative concerns?

You can only manage that balancing act if you have identified your prejudices in the planning stage of your correspondence.

Pressures

As a writer, you will always be affected by forces that come from within you and by forces that are completely outside of both yourself and the communication you are trying to write.

The inner forces are experienced as your needs, desires, beliefs, values, and preferences. These inner forces shape the WIIFM (What's In It For Me?) element of any written communication.

As with your reader, the outer forces come from culture and context. If you are not aware of them, you will inadvertently let these forces quietly make their presence known in your writing.

And so, once again, the issue is one of mindfulness. As part of preparation you need to ask yourself what outer forces are influencing your communication.

It's not a long process. Two simple questions will suffice:

"How are the values of the culture where I work relevant to this communication?"

"What recent events are affecting my feelings about this communication?"

Control can only occur within consciousness.

If you want to control the effect of your writing, be conscious of all the forces that are shaping your words.

Performance

So far, we have been discussing Preparation—the process by which we prepare our minds with the right understanding and attitudes. But before we move onto Planning, you will need to establish one thing about yourself.

Are you a procrastinator? Or are you a perfectionist? If you are unlucky, you might be both!

Over the years, I have developed and practiced a time-management system that I facetiously call Dynamic Procrastination—DP for short. It's easy to use. You accept any assignment, look at the due date, and then wait. I always wait until the deadline is looming and my colleagues are starting to panic. They know, from past experience, that I'll get the job done. But it's a double-edged sword. I have to wait until the force of despair, born of imminent disaster, propels me to my desk. Then, I work with extreme focus, energy, and concentration.

The beauty of DP is that, once I start, I work quickly and spontaneously. I depend on my creativity to get the words on the page.

The danger of DP is that it frequently doesn't allow for proper preparation and planning. It destroys teamwork and collaboration, and it's extremely tiring—I'm wrung out by the intensity, and my colleagues are exhausted by uncertainty and frustration. It's also dangerous. A lack of proper planning is always risky and, without it, the communication will rarely reach its optimum quality.

Perfectionists have a very different approach and experience.

It seems to me that perfectionists are better at managing their time and less likely to delay the start of their work. They are happy to undertake painstaking research and spend as much time as is necessary to organize their material and ensure that their structure is appropriate.

However, perfectionists don't have it easy. They can get bogged down in preparation and detail because they want everything to be perfect. This can destroy the flow of creativity that is essential to good writing.

Also, perfectionists want to get it right first time and, as we shall see, this is neither possible nor desirable.

In the worst case, you are a procrastinator and a perfectionist. This means you are going to give yourself the minimum time for the task and still expect the result to be brilliant. (Obviously you like pressure and are born to suffer and inflict suffering on those around you!)

Decide what you are. Don't fight it. You are what you are and this book isn't going to change it.

Managing your time

The amount of time you spend on a writing project will depend on three things: the importance of the communication, the complexity and length of the material, and the time available.

If your time is limited by a deadline, then you need to separate the task into its different phases and divide the available minutes, hours, or days accordingly.

If you have as much time as you want or need, then decide how long you are prepared to devote to the work. Do this at the outset. Ask yourself: how important is this communication? When must I have it finished?

Setting yourself a time limit may sound arbitrary, but it will help you stick to the process.

A surplus of time can be a burden—especially to perfectionists who will keep working and reworking the same phase and not proceed to the next. Procrastinators are mercifully free of this problem.

PREPARE	PLAN	DRAFT	REVIEW	REWRITE	POLISH
10%	30%	20%	10%	20%	10%

The percentage of time taken up by each stage of the process

Discipline, whether it is self-imposed or enforced by circumstance, will help you get the job done. Once you know how long you have, you are in a position to map out the use of your time.

The figure on the previous page looks at the stages in percentage terms of time available:

Preparation	**10%**
Planning	**30%**
Drafting	**20%**
Reviewing	**10%**
Rewriting	**20%**
Polishing	**10%**

The figure below looks at the same process in terms of a writer's hour.

Preparation	**6 minutes**
Planning	**18 minutes**
Drafting	**12 minutes**
Reviewing	**6 minutes**
Rewriting	**12 minutes**
Polishing	**6 minutes**

Broadly speaking, you spend 40% of your time in Planning and Preparation, and 60% of your time getting the words on the page in the way you want your reader to see them.

But only 20% of your time is spent working with a blank sheet of paper. The drafting phase is intentionally short. Once the correct planning has been done, drafting gets your thoughts on the page with the minimum of interruption and the maximum of flow. This process gives us the raw material of the communication. We still have 40% of our time to craft and polish it.

PREPARE	PLAN	DRAFT	REVIEW	REWRITE	POLISH
6 mins	18 mins	12 mins	6 mins	12 mins	6 mins

The percentages as portions of an hour

Summary and Action points

1. Before starting to write, review your own "4 Ps."
   - Personality
   - Prejudice
   - Pressures
   - Performance Style

2. What is your natural communication style? Are you:
   - A blue-headed analyst who wants to stick to the facts?
   - A green-headed organizer who concentrates on process?
   - A red-headed sensor who likes to focus on people?
   - A yellow-headed explorer who looks for creative opportunity?

3. What is your natural writing style? Know it and define it.

4. What Prejudices do you have about the subject and your reader that might be subtly affecting the tone and content of your communication?

5. What Pressures are affecting you? Consider the culture of your working environment, both formal and hidden, and the context of the communication.

6. What is your Performance style? Are you a procrastinator or a perfectionist?

7. Decide how long you will spend on completing the communication.

8. Break down the time available according to the timelines.

5. What is your purpose?

At one time or another, we've all been given the advice, "Think before you speak." That might kill spontaneity in a casual conversation, but it's good advice if you want your words to be taken seriously and remembered.

It applies just as well, if not better, to writing. "Think before you write." And yet, quite often, we don't.

In business, we sometimes start writing because we're under pressure. We are driven by a sense of obligation, necessity, and urgency. It may be that our inbox is overflowing and we know that people have been waiting for overdue replies. Or perhaps we have procrastinated and now find that an important letter that we wanted to write has become an urgent letter, and we must attend to it immediately.

This pressure can make us impetuous. Suddenly, what matters to us most is not writing a good letter, email, or memo but just getting the job done so that we can cross it off our To Do list and get back to work.

Such are the stresses and strains of corporate life. But we need to resist this temptation. You can save a lot of time and energy if you start every writing assignment by asking this simple question: "Why am I doing this?"

Most business correspondence tends to fall into three categories. We write to:

1. Inform
2. Persuade
3. Build a relationship

We appeal to the head, the heart, or the soul. It's important you know in which category your correspondence belongs. But that alone is not enough. These categories describe the task. They don't explain why you are doing it. Why you? What's in it for you? Before you even consider the content of a letter or email, you need to understand your own motivation and expectations.

WIIFM sounds like a radio station. It's not. It's an acronym for "What's In It For Me?"

You need to ask this question repeatedly until you have found your real reason for writing.

Let's look at an example. You are the manager of a department and, in the month of December, it falls upon you to write a staff memo to inform your team that, due to poor productivity, there will be no Christmas bonus this year.

Not a fun assignment, but one that needs to be done. Now, ask yourself, "What's In It For Me?" (WIIFM?).

You could say, "They need to be told and it's my responsibility." True.

But ask again, "What's In It For Me?" You could say, "I want to make sure that they receive a proper explanation. Only I can do that." Also true.

But ask yourself again, "What's In It For Me?" "They'll be disappointed and I don't want them to be demotivated." Fair enough.

WIIFM? "I don't want any of them to resign." Interesting.

WIIFM? "I don't want the hassle, the loss of time, or the expense of having to hire new people. I don't want to waste money on training new people. I don't want my bosses to think I'm mismanaging my department and allowing low morale to undermine the team's commitment. I don't want our competitors to smell blood and think we are in trouble, as things will then just get worse."

The more you think about it, the more you realize that there is quite a lot "in it for you."

The world of business has its own version of Abraham Maslow's hierarchy of needs. Corporate life instills six basic needs in most of us. They are:

1. The need to feel safe and secure
2. The need to look good
3. The need to feel good
4. The need to make money
5. The need to save money
6. The need to save time

If we look back at the "No bonus" memo we can feel the influence of these basic needs.

You won't feel safe and secure if your bosses think you are not motivating your department.

You won't look good if people start to quit on you.

You won't feel good if your team holds you responsible for a loss of income.

You won't make money if productivity is compromised by a loss of commitment.

You won't save money if you have to pay recruitment fees and then invest in training.

You won't save time if people leave. You'll be spending time searching to replace them.

The deeper you dig, the more of your own needs you will find. You need get to the bottom of them before you can ask the next critical question:

"What do I want my readers to do?"

When we write to someone, we are always trying to create a change in behavior. We want them to act, think, or feel differently. We want our writing to have an effect. We don't want them to read, understand, absorb, and forget it. We need a reaction to our words.

By forcing yourself to focus on the desired outcome of your communication, your writing will be more effective.

Let's go back to our memo. Let's assume that the most powerful need you experience is to feel safe and secure at a time when the company is struggling. You don't want your bosses to lose confidence in you.

What action would you like your readers to take?

You might want them to write back and give an assurance that they understand your position, do not hold you responsible, and intend to stick with the team in the certainty that business will pick up. Or you might want them to write to the heads of the organization and question their decisions and not yours.

You might want them to set up individual meetings with you to discuss the matter more personally so that you can give them necessary reassurances.

You might want them to attend an open meeting to discuss the matter.

Whatever your desired outcome, it will have a profound effect on the way in which you write the memo. It will affect its intent, content, structure, tone of voice, style, opening, and closing.

Let's go to extremes to illustrate the point. Let's assume that you have a completely different basic need. You want to save money. The company is not doing well. Cost-cutting measures will soon be introduced. Paying out severance packages is expensive but you feel downsizing is necessary. In an ideal world, some of your staff will resign and save you that cost.

So what is your purpose? You want the less committed, the less energetic, and the less productive to either change their work ethic dramatically or to tender their resignation.

What exactly do you want them to do? You want them to talk to you personally and make a decision about their future.

A very different memo is required. Let's look at them both:

To: Division A
From: You
Subject: A tough year

Dear Team,

This has been a tough year and I congratulate you all for prevailing under such difficult circumstances.

It's thanks to your hard work and commitment that we have survived and are in a position to move forward.

But unfortunately our numbers are down. Our profits are more than 15% beneath our targets. And after long conversations with our senior management, I regret to say that none of us will receive a Christmas bonus this year.

I know this is a disappointment for all of you and a real financial blow for some of you. I'd like to do whatever I can to help and discuss this with each of you personally. Please speak to my assistant to arrange a time in my schedule that is convenient.

I'd like to stress that this downturn is temporary.

If we can maintain the energy and momentum you have built in the last two or three months, I am sure we will get back on track and I will be in a position to lobby senior management for a mid-term bonus next year.

I can't make promises, but I do feel confident.

Until then, keep up the good work and try to see me before the end of next week.

Sincerely,

You

The task of this memo is to deliver bad news. No bonus. The purpose of the memo is to maintain the team's commitment and make sure that anyone who is really struggling knows that they can come and see you. The action you require is that they speak to your assistant and arrange a time.

Now let's look at the same news in the service of a different purpose.

To: Division A
From: You
Subject: Bonus

As you all know, it's been a tough year. In some areas we have performed well, and in others we have failed to reach our targets. As a result, our figures are down by 15%.
After long talks with senior management, I regret to say that we will not be able to award a Christmas bonus this year.

I know this is a severe disappointment for those of you who have worked hard throughout these last 12 months. And I value your energy and commitment highly. However, our output is judged as a team effort. Therefore, we are all adversely affected.

To prepare us for the renewed effort we must make next year, I would like to meet with each of you personally to review your performance and discuss your objectives. Please speak to my assistant to book a time in my schedule.

I'm determined that we face this challenge knowing that everyone in the team is giving 100% of their effort.

Please ensure we meet before the end of next week. I look forward to our discussion.

Sincerely,

You

Once again, the task of the memo is to deliver bad news. No bonus. The purpose of the memo is to make your belief clear—some members of the team are performing well and some are not. The direct action you require is that they arrange a performance review so that you can sort the wheat from the chaff.

These two memos contain similar information but are written with a very different tone of voice. That difference is explained entirely by purpose. And once you have defined your purpose, you'll be able to stipulate exactly what actions you want your readers to take.

Every aspect of your writing will be affected by these decisions, which is why they must be made at the very start of the process—before you develop a strategy, before you gather information, before you do anything.

> One possible result of investigating your purpose is that you'll decide to write nothing. Or maybe you'll decide to reach your audience through a different medium—a phone call, a meeting, or an intermediary.

Only when you know your purpose and desired outcome, can you really develop a communication strategy and decide how you are going to deliver your message.

Once your purpose is clear, the cornerstone of your plan is in place.

Summary and Action points

You can't plan any form of correspondence until you know three things.

1. The Task: are you informing, persuading, or building a relationship with your reader? Are you appealing to their heads, hearts, or souls?

2. The Purpose: why are you doing this? What's in it for you? (WIIFM?) What benefit can you derive from this communication? What is your motivation?

3. What is the desired outcome? What exactly do you want your readers to do? (Not what do you want them to think or feel; what action do you want them to take?)

4. Ask yourself this question: "Now that I know what I want them to do, is writing the best way to make them do it?"

Exercise

You are writing to your colleagues to inform them that there is a change of venue for the annual conference. Think of ten different outcomes, ten possible actions you might want them to take as a result of reading your message.

6. Communication strategy

By this stage in the process you will understand your reader, yourself, and the way in which you both like to communicate. This means you can get on the right wavelength and deliver your message in a style that will be easy to read and absorb without distortion.

You also know exactly what you want your reader to do.

So you are now ready to design a communication strategy that will bring you together in agreement on your desired outcome.

But there's still some groundwork you need to do before you start to collect and organize your information. You need to:

● Establish the nature of the task
● Identify the obstacles and barriers
● Build a frame for your argument
● Determine the level of formality
● Choose the appropriate medium
● Set the tone of the communication

Identifying the Task

The figure opposite is a matrix that will help you establish the challenge you are facing. It's based on two axes—Hard to Easy, and Positive to Negative (For You or Against You).

The Hard to Easy axis is a measure of how difficult it would be for your reader to comply with your request and do what you want. This is not a measure of whether they want your desired outcome. It's a measure of whether or not they are in a position to help you achieve it.

The Positive to Negative axis is a measure of how they feel about your proposal. Are they supportive or hostile to your suggestions and recommendations? Are they for you or against you?

The matrix is easy to use. Start with the horizontal axis. First ask, "Is the reader for or against me?" Mark the answer from 1 to 10, where 1 means they are for you and 10 means they are opposed. Or 1 is positive and 10 is extremely negative.

Now move to the vertical axis and mark your answer from 1 to 10, where 1 means it is hard for them to do as you ask and 10 means it is easy.

Draw a horizontal line from your mark on the vertical axis and a vertical line from your mark on the horizontal axis. The intersection point of these two lines tells you which of the four boxes describes your writing task.

Blue Box

Your reader is on your side and finds it easy to comply with your request or recommendation. This is the easy box. Given such a positive predisposition, your communication can be short but must stick to the point and contain all the necessary facts to enable your reader to take action. The tone should be warm and positive.

Green Box

Your reader is supportive but there are difficulties. Something is getting in the way. It's not easy for them to do as you ask. When faced with this situation, your communication needs to be helpful. It will need to be longer and contain a solution to their problem. You may have to focus on a process that overcomes the obstacle. Your tone needs to be warm and supportive.

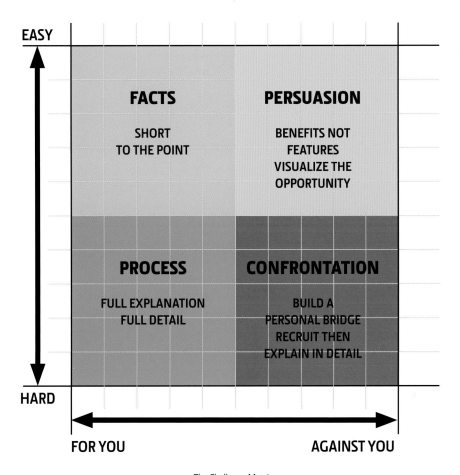

The Challenge Matrix

Red Box

You're in trouble here. Your reader is neither for you nor in a position to do as you suggest. It's tempting to say that this is an impossible situation. But that's not necessarily so. The best approach is to deal with the emotional issue first. Until you have overcome that, the reader will always hide behind the obstacle and continue to blow you off. Your tone needs to be understanding and conciliatory.

Yellow Box

You'll need to be persuasive. Your reader is in a position to comply but does not feel positively toward you. You must change that. You need to overcome resistance by selling the benefits of your proposal. You need to excite their imagination so that they can see the value of your point of view and recommendation. Your tone needs to be inspiring and persuasive.

You may notice a superficial similarity between the arrangements and color-coding of this matrix and the HBDI model. This is purely coincidental but, nonetheless, helpful as a mnemonic.

In the blue box you need to be brief and stick to the facts. In the green box you need to explain the process. In the red box you need to address emotional issues. In the yellow box you have to focus on opportunity and inspire the reader's imagination.

Once you have established the nature of the task, you can be a little more specific.

Obstacles and Barriers

If your intersection point is in the blue box, heave a sigh of relief. But if you find yourself in the green, red, or yellow boxes, then something is getting in your way. There is an obstacle or barrier.

If it's a green box task, then you have a supportive audience who's got a problem. You need to identify exactly what it is. Your correspondence needs to do more than acknowledge it, you need to help your reader address the problem and find a solution. As part of your planning, write down everything you know about the obstacle you and your reader have to overcome.

If it's a yellow or red box, then you have a reader who is not supportive. In either instance, you need to identify the reason why they feel negatively about you or your proposal. Write it down.

The red box is double trouble. You have two problems to solve—emotional resistance and practical difficulties. If you are going to take on this daunting task, you need to list all of the obstacles in your path so that you can develop a communication strategy.

The key to this exercise is to be specific. Don't write, "He doesn't like me." Write down why. Don't write, "She'll find it hard to get internal support for my proposal." Write down the exact nature of the opposition she'll face.

You will never get support for a specific proposal if you think and talk about it in general terms.

Frame Analysis

Creating a frame around your argument is a powerful way of directing your reader to your desired outcome. This concept is not new. Aristotle called it *atechnoi* and Cicero called it *stasis*.

It has been defined as "a psychological device that offers a perspective and manipulates salience in order to influence subsequent judgment."

Essentially, it's a way of putting your argument or proposition into a context that separates it from counter-arguments.

Kelton Rhoads cites some interesting examples at his website, workingpsychology.com.

A case of reframing that captured the attention of the world was the trial of O. J. Simpson for murder. The legal frame of the debate was simple—innocent versus guilty. But each lawyer fought hard to reframe the argument and sway the court. The prosecution frame was strong male wife-beater versus weak female victim; the defense team tried to create a frame of ethnic minority victim versus racist white police force. The surprising outcome was probably best explained by the way in which the defense's frame narrowed the jury's options. Within that frame, there was only one plausible verdict as the police were clearly shown to be racist. Innocent.

Rhoads looks at three types of framing that we frequently experience in everyday life—reframing, focus framing, and contrast framing.

Imagine you are going into an electronics store to look at DVD players. You haven't decided if you do or don't want one. The frame of the opportunity is simply DVD player versus no DVD player. But if a salesman approaches you, he may engage you in a conversation about the mind-numbing garbage that is transmitted every day on TV. However, he'll point out that a DVD player allows you to view only what you want to see—no advertising, no game shows, no fake reality programs, and so on.

> Suddenly the decision has been reframed. You are no longer choosing between DVD or no DVD. You are choosing between cinema and television—an easier choice.

If you buy a healthy breakfast bar, it might proudly claim on the wrapper to be 95% fat-free. This is a case of focus framing. Your attention is focused on the positive, and consequently, you feel favorably toward the product. Were you to resist this focus framing, you might alert yourself to the ugly fact that 5% of the bar, perhaps one bite, is pure fat and nothing but fat. You'd feel differently. Would you buy a bar that proclaimed it was 5% pure fat? Probably not.

> Contrast framing is an old ploy of the door-to-door encyclopedia salesman, but it can be used to minimize the apparent cost of any expensive item. The salesman makes his pitch and, when the prospective buyer balks at the expense, he then offers payment terms over a long period of time. For example, he might offer $1,000 worth of books at a rate of $20 per month over five years. (You'll notice he's already made an extra $200.) This doesn't sound too painful. But if he reframes that figure he could build an argument that says the outlay is only 64 cents a day. That is less than you'd spend on a can of cola.

The contrast framing occurs when you set the cost of a cola a day against the value of your child's education. Only the most miserly parent would deny their child such a small investment.

This actually happened to me quite recently. American Express offered me a health insurance policy over the phone. They wanted $36 per month. The salesman pointed out that it was just over a dollar a day—not enough to buy a cup of coffee!

> Once you have decided on your purpose and know your desired outcome, ask yourself how you might frame your argument to narrow your reader's options. Can you present those options in such a way that whatever your reader chooses will be acceptable to you?

This can work on a very basic level. Some years ago, I found myself attending meetings with a particularly persistent insurance broker whom I would have preferred to avoid. But somehow he kept luring me to his office. Eventually, a salesman friend explained the tactic to me. The invitations, made in writing or over the phone, would never be as simple as, "Are you available on Tuesday 10th?" They would always contain an option such as, "Which is more convenient to you, Tuesday 10th or Thursday 12th?" Invariably, I would delay the inevitable and take the later date. I had been given a choice and took the lesser of two evils. But to the broker, either of these evils was perfectly acceptable. The choice was illusory, the outcome was determined by the broker.

Formality

There are three variables to consider when deciding how formal your correspondence should be. They are:

1. **The personal relationship with your reader**
2. **The professional relationship with your reader**
3. **The appeal of your correspondence to your reader**

The illustration below is a calculator to help you establish the Formality Factor of your communication. It works by asking you to answer and score three questions.

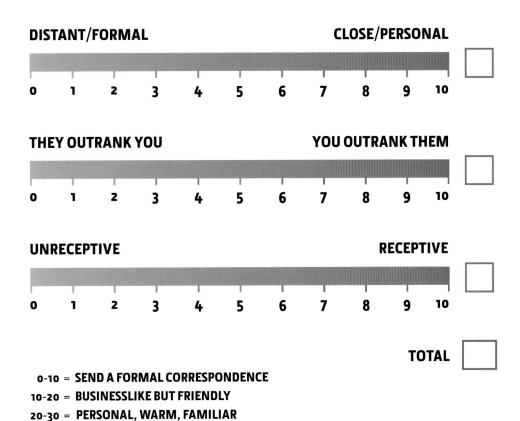

DISTANT/FORMAL   **CLOSE/PERSONAL**

0 1 2 3 4 5 6 7 8 9 10

THEY OUTRANK YOU   **YOU OUTRANK THEM**

0 1 2 3 4 5 6 7 8 9 10

UNRECEPTIVE   **RECEPTIVE**

0 1 2 3 4 5 6 7 8 9 10

TOTAL

0-10 = **SEND A FORMAL CORRESPONDENCE**
10-20 = **BUSINESSLIKE BUT FRIENDLY**
20-30 = **PERSONAL, WARM, FAMILIAR**

The first is, "How close are you to your reader? Is it a close and personal relationship or is it a distant and formal relationship?" The hot end of the bar represents close and the cool end represents distant. Score the question by deciding where on the bar the relationship sits. For example, someone you know well and with whom you occasionally socialize would score a high number, perhaps a 9 or 10. While the colleague you occasionally chat with at the water cooler may only rate a 5. And the client you rarely see would be down at the 1 or 2 end of the scale.

The next question is, "Are you above or below them on the corporate ladder? Do you look up to them or do they look up to you?" If you are higher, give yourself a high mark. If you feel equal to your reader, score it a 5. If you are writing to someone that you hold in high esteem, mark it down at the blue end of the scale.

This second question appears crude and ego driven. It's not. It's intended to reveal a subtle protocol in business writing. When we address people who have risen to a high rank, we show respect by displaying a certain level of formality. On the other hand, when people of high standing write to the people who respect them, that same protocol suggests a more friendly tone to soften any sense of authority that is merely derived from status.

The last question is, "Will they like what I'm writing, or will they hate it?" If they are going to like it, score it highly at the hot end of the scale. If it's unwelcome news, score it down near the cool end.

Then add up the three scores. The legend at the bottom gives you an analysis of the results. Basically, 0–10 suggests you need to be formal, 10–20 suggests a businesslike but friendly tone of voice, and 20–30 means you can use a very personal style.

Once you know the Formality Factor, you can choose the appropriate medium.

Media

Below is a hierarchy of media rated from the most formal at the top to the least formal at the bottom.

1. **Personal Letter**
2. **Quality printed materials with signed cover note**
   (proposals, legal documents, company reports)
3. **Attachment to an email**
4. **Email**
5. **Handwritten notes**
6. **Cheap printed materials without cover note**
   (newsletters, flyers)
7. **CC email**
8. **BCC email**

In this day and age of digital communication, a letter—one that is sent on quality stock and bears a printed letterhead—remains the most formal and the most personal type of correspondence. Nothing else comes close.

But we receive so few letters these days that they are starting to feel rare, almost precious.

That's not to say their value is explained by scarcity. A letter has some unique attributes. While the writing style can be formal, the fact that it is signed by hand makes a letter feel personal and direct. (A typed signature or a "pp" by an assistant ruins the effect entirely.) And although a letter can be copied and sent to more than one recipient, it feels exclusive and private—perhaps because it arrives in a sealed envelope.

And on a purely emotional level, a letter is a tangible, real-world manifestation of the writer's communication, while an email belongs in a digital universe that seems almost abstract by comparison. Even if you print an email, it will never have the substance, gravitas, or formality of a letter.

Slightly lower on the formality scale, you'll find expensive printed materials—legal documents, company reports, or business proposals. These are obviously less private, as they are intended for circulation. But they can still be personalized by including a signed cover note.

If you want to send formal correspondence electronically, then the best way is to create a separate document for your message and then add it as an attachment to an email. This seems to work like a "virtual" letter. It manages to appropriate some of the personal and formal values of a printed letter while using the email as both a cover note and faster delivery mechanism.

The problem with email is that the medium is becoming inherently casual.

This is reflected in the language and writing styles that email seems to encourage—salutations are frequently omitted, correct grammar ignored, and punctuation seems to be a thing of the past. While this may create a sense of immediacy, it does so at the cost of formality. This is likely to get worse. PDA email systems and SMS text messages are encouraging abbreviation to the point of developing an entirely new vocabulary. It can be effective, fast, and personal, but never formal.

Similarly, handwritten notes can be personal but lack formality. You may find them useful for "blue box" communication, where your reader is supportive and able to comply with your request. Elsewhere, they may be less appropriate.

And finally, at the very bottom of the scale, you'll find cheap printed materials and the most impersonal medium of all—the "CC" email.

Cheap printed materials are clearly made for mass circulation—newsletters, flyers, and so on. They are impersonal, usually unimpressive, and destined for the garbage.

The CC email may be personal to the addressee but not to those who are merely copied in on the correspondence. Given that we are all buried under a plethora of electronic communication, many people now have a policy of only skimming through "CC" emails and rarely, if ever, respond to them.

The exception to this rule is the "BCC" that suggests collusion between the sender and the hidden, secret recipient. A BCC is furtive and personal but not formal. Personally, I find them rather sneaky and would advise against using them.

Most of us have the habit of replying to correspondence in the medium in which we receive it.

If you send me an email, as likely as not I'll hit "Reply" and send you one back. It's worth questioning this reflex. If I send you an email and you want to reply in a very formal tone, you can always send me a letter. Just switching the medium makes quite a powerful statement. Or you might decide to call, and not write, as you want to create a sense of urgency or appear more personal.

> Whatever you choose, the medium will make a statement about the formality of your communication irrespective of its content.

Summary and Action points

1. Determine the task of your communication. Is this a blue, green, red, or yellow box issue?

2. Identify any obstacles or barriers to either comprehension or compliance.

3. Frame your argument. Create a perspective that focuses your reader's attention on your desired outcome.

4. Work out the necessary Formality Factor of your correspondence.

5. Choose a medium that is appropriate to the level of formality you require.

Exercise

Take a recent piece of communication and do the following:

1. Decide where it belongs on the "task matrix." Which color?

2. Reframe the argument or request.

7. Gathering information

You have established your purpose and desired outcome—these will serve as the DNA of your writing. You understand the nature of the task, have identified the obstacles and barriers, and have framed your argument accordingly. You've also assessed the necessary level of formality and chosen an appropriate medium.

And yet you still haven't committed a word to paper! That's good. You're only a little more than half way through the "Planning" phase. At the moment, you should only be making notes.

You are now ready to collect and organize the information that will put meat on the bones of your communication.

To do that, we're going to look at how to mind map your purpose and use a process we call "Claim, Value, Proof" to make sure you differentiate between the claims you make and the benefits they offer. As we shall see,

claims may matter to you but it's their benefits that will really appeal to your reader.

Mind Mapping

Mind mapping is a technique invented by Tony Buzan, who has written many manuals and books on the subject. There are many versions of the concept—I've seen "Spidergrams" and "Hub & Spoke" diagrams, for example. But I think mind maps are the most highly evolved version of this idea.

Originally, Buzan developed the system as a memory aid—he was trying to find a better way of taking study notes at college. But since then, it has proved to be a very useful tool for creative thinking and for organizing information.

While our thinking tends to be random, our writing needs to be linear.

We must lead our reader from one point to the next within a structure that maintains his or her focus on the argument we are developing.

The beauty of a mind map is that it enables us to take a mass of undifferentiated and poorly organized information and arrange it in such a way that it is meaningful to our purpose.

In fact a mind map puts our purpose at the very center of our thinking and then relates everything we know directly to it. By doing this, we get a bird's-eye view of everything we know and can immediately decide what information and ideas are relevant and necessary and what thoughts and information we should exclude.

good for nervous system

SLEEP

sleep deeper

wake refresh

sleep longer

no hangovers

less beer

HEALTH

DIET

cardiovascula system

lower cholesterol

lower pul

appetite suppressant

me time

RELAXATION

time out from wor

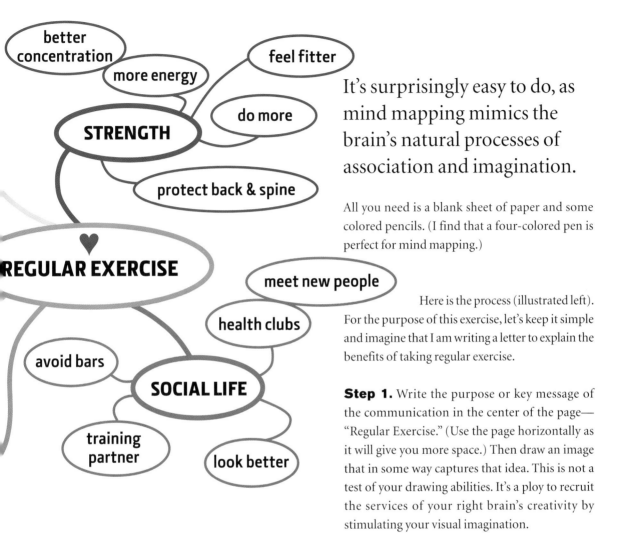

It's surprisingly easy to do, as mind mapping mimics the brain's natural processes of association and imagination.

All you need is a blank sheet of paper and some colored pencils. (I find that a four-colored pen is perfect for mind mapping.)

Here is the process (illustrated left). For the purpose of this exercise, let's keep it simple and imagine that I am writing a letter to explain the benefits of taking regular exercise.

Step 1. Write the purpose or key message of the communication in the center of the page— "Regular Exercise." (Use the page horizontally as it will give you more space.) Then draw an image that in some way captures that idea. This is not a test of your drawing abilities. It's a ploy to recruit the services of your right brain's creativity by stimulating your visual imagination.

Step 2. Draw four or five branches that radiate out from the center. Make them wavy and organic, not straight and lifeless. Make each branch a different color. This will also stimulate your imagination and color-code the different strands of your thinking. You'll find this will be helpful later.

Step 3. Think about "Regular Exercise" and add the first four or five keywords that occur to you. What are the big themes of the subject? Put them at the end of the branches you have drawn. As you'll see, I chose Health, Strength, Sleep, and Relaxation. Later I realized that Regular Exercise could also stimulate a Social Life and so I added a new branch.

Step 4. Go to the end of each branch and treat it as if it were the center of the page. Radiate out from each of the keywords and add further branches of relevant thoughts and ideas. Let the map grow. Let new thoughts trigger more new thoughts and keep adding them until the branches are full and nothing more is occurring to you.

By the end of this process, you will have transferred everything you know about the subject to the page.

But unlike a list of thoughts, information, and ideas, a mind map groups everything into themes.

Each one of the themes relates directly to the purpose of your correspondence. While a mind map allows you to track your neural pathways and visualize your thinking, it also allows your thoughts to find new pathways. In this sense, mind mapping stimulates creativity. All you have to do is connect the ends of the branches and see what new ideas occur.

For example, in my mind map on Regular Exercise, I could arbitrarily connect Diet and Social Life and explore the idea of meeting friends at a health food café. Or I could connect Diet and Sleep and explore the idea of eating foods that are known to promote relaxation before going to bed. Each mind map contains a thousand opportunities to build pathways that the mind would otherwise have ignored, as you can choose to build connections that would not naturally occur through the process of association.

As new thoughts occur, attach them to the branch where they most obviously belong, or create a new branch.

At the end of the process, you will have an overview of everything you know that has been organized into a set of themes and sub-themes. And they'll all be color-coded. You'll find it's much easier to keep this information in mind now that you have gone through the process of visualizing it.

You now have the raw material of your communication, but before you can use it, we need to refine it.

Claim, Value, Proof

There's usually a big difference between claims and benefits. A claim might seem valuable to you but be of little interest to your reader.

> For example, let's assume that I make gadgets and can rightfully claim that my gadgets are known throughout the world. They are the most famous gadgets on the planet. I could even substantiate that claim by saying, "Research has proven that over 70% of the civilized world has heard of our gadgets." Sounds impressive.

However, this is a claim and must be translated into a benefit if it is to be motivating as well as impressive.

> Much of the information on your mind map will be in the form of claims, ideas, and facts. Before we can use any of it, we need to subject it to a process we call Claim, Value, Proof.

Back to my gadgets. We'll assume that I am writing to a retailer who doesn't yet stock them. What is the value of their fame to my reader? To explore the possibilities we need to swap perspectives and ask a simple question.

> Look at the claim through your reader's eyes and ask, "What's in it for me?"

My claim: "My gadgets are world famous." Reader response: "WIIFM?"

My revised claim: "Because they are famous, people trust them." Reader response: "Really. WIIFM?"

My next revised claim: "They buy them because they trust them." Reader response: "Lucky you. WIIFM?"

My next revised claim: "You can sell more of our gadgets because of their good reputation." Reader response: "Interesting. WIIFM?"

My next revised claim: "The more you sell the better deal you can negotiate with me. You'll increase your profit margin and make more money." Reader response: "Send a truckload. We're in business."

> We've found the value of the claim and established the benefit—make money. We could have saved ourselves a lot of conversation if we had originally presented the claim as: "Our gadgets will increase your profitability. Their worldwide reputation makes them easy to sell in high volume at a high mark-up."

If your communication is to be persuasive, then every claim you make has to have a value to your reader.

As we have already noted, there are six core values and motivators in business life. They are:

1. **Make money**
2. **Save money**
3. **Save time**
4. **Look good**
5. **Feel good**
6. **Feel secure**

When your reader asks "WIIFM?" he or she will want to see that the claim leads to one of these six benefits.

But the benefit alone is not enough. You have to prove it.

Saying it is so doesn't make it so. Unless your readers have such faith and trust in your opinion that they believe every word you say, you must substantiate your claims with irrefutable evidence.

In business, we find there are several stock approaches to validating your claims and benefits. They are:

1. **Case studies**
2. **Testimonials**
3. **Expert quotes**
4. **Facts and statistics**
5. **Visual images**
6. **Demonstration**

It's important to remove any trace of personal bias. Case studies should be endorsed by a reputable third party whenever possible, testimonials cannot come from people on your payroll, experts must be acknowledged within their field, facts must be checked, and sources cited. Visual images and demonstrations offer your readers the security of being observers and trusting their own judgment and not yours.

I have always felt that testimonials are potentially weak and the most susceptible to skepticism. I remember an airline advertising campaign that printed glowing references from passengers. Underneath each was a credit that read, "This is an authentic passenger statement." This device undermined the credibility of the statements and forced the reader to question whether they were genuinely unbiased or sponsored by the airline's agency.

As noted earlier, saying it is so doesn't make it so. If you are going to get someone else to say it, make sure they are clearly independent and credible.

Once you have mind mapped your information, and ensured your claims contain motivating benefits that can be proven, you have reached the penultimate stage of the planning process.

Before we start writing, we'll look at structure.

Summary and Action points

1. Draw a mind map that organizes everything you know around your Purpose or main theme.

2. Look at any claims you would like to make and subject them to the Claim, Value, Proof process. Ask WIIFM? as many times as it takes to find the benefit to your reader.

3. Find irrefutable proof for any of the benefits and claims that you intend to include in your correspondence.

Exercise

1. Mind map the word "Success."

2. Take just one of the claims you frequently make in business. Ask WIIFM? as many times as it takes to find the benefit to your customer.

8. Choosing a structure

You are almost ready to write.

In the Preparation phase, you have considered how both you and your reader like to communicate—you can now avoid a clash of styles and make sure you are on the right wavelength.

In the Planning phase, you have clearly stated your Purpose and developed a communication strategy. You have organized your information into a mind map and have subjected it to a grueling "WIIFM?" to ensure that it contains benefits and not simply the sort of claims your company habitually makes.

The very last stage of planning is to choose a structure. I can think of ten different structures that are commonly used in business writing. Each serves a particular purpose or task.

They are:

Problem/Solution	**To make a recommendation**
Cause/Effect	**To explain**
Chronology	**To defend or recruit**
Narrative	**To review**
Process	**To instruct**
Comparison	**To analyze**
Journalism	**To inform**
Top and Tail	**To deliver bad news**
Q & A	**To clarify**
The Diamond	**To persuade**

We'll look at all of these in turn and then focus on the last one—the Diamond. This structure contains a process that is derived from Aristotle's principles of rhetoric and is designed to make your writing more persuasive. If your purpose is to motivate a change of behavior, or if you want to make a strong recommendation, the Diamond is almost certainly the tool you'll need.

But, as we shall see, it's possible to use some of the other structures to good effect within the Diamond. We'll get to that later.

For the purpose of demonstrating the ten structures, let's create a simple situation that would require different types of correspondence to be sent to different stakeholders within a company.

Let's imagine you work for a medium-sized company that occupies two or three floors of a high-rise building. You are the office manager and responsible for the office resources—you have a budget that covers the purchase and maintenance of all equipment. When you need additional funds, you lobby the board of directors.

Recently, a mobile coffee station called Mister Barista opened in your neighborhood. A couple of enterprising local kids are now selling much better coffee than the dishwater brew you provide in the machines at the end of each corridor. This is causing a problem. Understandably, your staff are taking time out to go down to the coffee stand and get themselves a decent cup of coffee. This has far-reaching implications and effects—loss of time, phones unanswered, employees complaining they have to pay top dollar for their coffee because the company doesn't provide for them.

You, as office manager, are sure to become embroiled in this problem. Let's see how the different structures might be of use to you in their most basic forms.

Problem/Solution–To Make a Recommendation

The Problem/Solution structure is a favorite of management consultancies because it provides a very direct route to a recommendation. It comprises two simple steps:

1. State the problem
2. Explain a course of action that solves it

The danger of this approach lies in the way you state the problem. If you and your readers don't share an understanding of the situation, you'll lose them immediately and be unlikely to gain support for your recommendation.

As office manager, here's how you might use the Problem/Solution structure in a note to the board:

Dear Board,

As I am sure you are all aware, we've seen a dramatic increase in the number of complaints we are receiving about staff being away from their desks. The explanation is simple. They are all down at the Mister Barista coffee stand.

The only way for us to reverse this trend is to provide better coffee for our employees.

I recommend that we update our vending machines on all floors and undercut the local competition by only charging a dollar a cup. As you'll see from the attached spreadsheet, we'll recover our costs in 18 months, Mister Barista will be long gone and everyone will be back to work.

Sincerely,

You

Crude, I admit. But I hope it illustrates the simple structure. It also raises an issue. What if the board thinks that the problem is not the quality of the coffee but the fact that staff members have nowhere to socialize and chat? That's why they are going to Mister Barista. If this is the case, then your recommendation will fall flat. This structure only works if you have identified the true problem and not just a symptom of a deeper, underlying issue.

Cause/Effect–To Give an Explanation

The board writes to you and asks why everyone is suddenly moaning about the coffee machines.

Dear Board,

I too have been inundated with complaints about the coffee machines.

The problem dates back to October when Mister Barista opened their coffee stand at the end of Corporation Avenue. They are serving excellent cappuccinos and lattes at a very competitive price. Sadly, our own offering does not compare favorably and so many of the staff are now leaving the office two or three times a day.

Given the time it takes to get there and back, time spent in line and then time spent chatting to other staff, we're probably losing an hour of productivity per day per employee.

As a result the switchboard is overloaded with messages, personal assistants are struggling to schedule meetings, and clients are complaining.

I fear the situation will continue until action is taken.

Sincerely,

You

Cause/Effect doesn't require a recommendation, just an explanation.

The board can decide to upgrade the coffee machines. On the other hand they might encourage staff to take their cellphones to the stand and remain in constant touch—it's up to them. There are any number of options they can consider.

Chronology—To Defend or Recruit

A new member of the board has noticed the deserted atmosphere of the offices and asks why someone hasn't had the good sense to install some decent coffee machines.

Dear New Board Member,

We moved into this building in October 2004. At the time, our budgets were constrained by the necessary refurbishments we needed to undertake. The larger part of our available funds was dedicated to IT.

We did consider upgrading the coffee machines. However, our contract with the Mean Bean Company was not due for review until January 2005. At the year-end board meeting, it was decided to renew the contract for another 24 months, as there had been no serious complaints.

It wasn't until October 2005 that Mister Barista started its operation and lured our staff from the building.

We can reconsider our arrangements with the Mean Bean Company in December and take appropriate action.

Sincerely,

You

Chronology provides an excellent and clear explanation that can either act as a defense of actions that have failed or as a recruitment drive for a change of strategy. If you want someone to help you in the future, explain what happened in the past. Chronology brings a sense of objectivity as it can focus on events without getting mired down in responsibilities and missed opportunities. **Chronology establishes a "This is what happened" platform for a debate about what should be done.**

Narrative—To Review

Narrative is a more personal form of Chronology and one that puts the writer in the first person. Narrative is an invitation to review the writer's role in events.

In this instance, there is a subtle change in your reason for writing—the new board member is asking why YOU didn't do something about the situation. After all, you are the office manager.

Dear New Board Member,

I'd like to give you some background on what is now being called "The Great Coffee Machine Fiasco."

We moved here in October 2004. Our new landlords provided coffee facilities as part of our rental agreement. I reviewed our contract with the Mean Bean Company and, as there had been no complaints, decided to renew it. We extended for 24 months.

I was surprised when Mister Barista appeared on the corner of Corporation Avenue in October 2005. The quality of their coffee, combined with their loyalty card, secured the immediate patronage of our staff, and we have suffered a mass exodus ever since.

At the December board meeting, I would like to present a proposal that will rid us of both Mean Bean and Mister Barista and keep our staff fully caffeinated and happily at their desks.

Sincerely,

You

Narrative has a tendency to be personal while Chronology leans more to the impersonal. By writing a narrative you are inviting your reader to reflect and comment on your personal involvement in events.

Process—To Instruct

The clearest way to give instructions is to establish a step-by-step process that explains how you need people to act.

In this case, the new board member has decided you must replace the existing coffee machines with superior models.

Dear New Board Member,

I applaud your decision to install new coffee machines. To expedite the matter, we'll need to do the following:

1. Find a new hardware supplier and establish a cost and delivery date.

2. Inform our landlords of the date that we'd like them to remove the existing machines.

3. Cancel our contract with the Mean Bean Company and appoint a new and better supplier. The "True Brew Company" is highly recommended.

4. Instigate an internal PR campaign that tells the staff we are going to be providing the best cup of coffee on either side of Corporation Avenue.

5. Establish a price point that quickly puts Mister Barista out of business.

I'll get back to you with a detailed timeline.

Sincerely,

You

Once a process has been established, it's easier to manage the details as they can be organized within their relevant stages. Take the process away and the details will quickly unravel and spread into chaos. Process also makes it easier to assign roles to the different people responsible for ensuring the job gets done.

Comparison—To Analyze

Comparison is a very effective tool for analysis. But be careful. **A comparison must always be fair.** If you compare your preferred course of action with one that is deliberately impractical, your personal bias will be clearly on display and this will undermine the validity of your argument. Comparison works best on a level playing field.

In this case, the board of directors want to know their options.

Dear Board,

We need to make a decision. We can either install new coffee machines and upgrade the coffee we provide, or we can allow the staff to patronize Mister Barista and develop ways of using it as a working space. One possibility would be to install some tables there with wireless Internet connectivity and insist on the use of call forwarding to mobile phones.

INSTALLING NEW MACHINES

The Positives:
* *We provide better coffee and fewer staff will leave the building*
* *We show that we are sensitive to staff needs and requirements*
* *New machines will be profitable after two years*

The Negatives:
* *High initial investment*
* *Impossible to beat Mister Barista on quality*
* *High risk of failure. Staff enjoy the break and the coffee outside*

THE MISTER BARISTA VIRTUAL OFFICE

The Positives:
• Low initial investment
• We show that we are sensitive to staff need and requirements
• In keeping with modern business trends—we look progressive
• Staff get the coffee they want

The Negatives:
• Encourages disruption to working day and might reduce productivity
• Potential of this system being abused by staff

On the basis of this comparison, I recommend we allow a three-month trial of the "Virtual Office." If it doesn't work, we have a very simple fallback position. What do you think?

Sincerely,

You

Fair comparison is a very effective technique for "framing" your argument, as it allows you to control the options and variables within the decision-making process. But if you fail to include obvious and reasonable options, it's most likely to backfire on you and your recommendation will be rejected.

Journalism—To Inform

The American Heritage Dictionary defines journalism in these words: "The style of writing characteristic of material in newspapers and magazines, consisting of direct presentation of facts or occurrences with little attempt at analysis or interpretation."

When writing in the journalistic style, your intent is to report the facts without bias. There is no desired outcome other than to inform. You don't want to encourage any particular course of action. You have no agenda.

In the case of the coffee crisis, the board may ask you to write a piece for the company newsletter that looks at the Mister Barista phenomenon. Here goes:

Some of you walking down Corporation Avenue may have been surprised by the number of colleagues you encounter sitting at the tables outside the Apex Building.

Enticed by the exquisite aromas of Mister Barista's coffee wagon, they have unwittingly become a part of our latest experiment in off-site working.

When George and his brother Andrew set up their mobile café in October of last year, no one could have imagined that they would become a second nerve center of our own operation.

But their coffee and pastries have proved to be so popular that our management has now installed extra tables and an Internet station to make sure staff can stay at work even when they are out of the office.

With mobile phones and Internet access, it will be interesting to see who has the greatest pull during the winter months—hot coffee or a warm office.

The journalistic style, within business communication, is intended to be non-judgmental. It reports and informs. And depending on the medium, it can be used to entertain.

Top and Tail—To Deliver Bad News

The top and tail format is intended to soften the blow of bad news by starting and ending on a positive note. It's a very common device for rejection letters but can be put to good use in any situation where you have to deliver a disappointing response but want to maintain motivation and morale.

> Let's assume the board has turned down a request to subsidize the coffee at Mister Barista. Your job is to inform the staff's highly agitated caffeine addicts who were hoping for a cheap coffee buzz.

To: All staff
From: You
Subject: **Mister Barista**

The board met last night to discuss the proposal that we subsidize the coffee down at Mister Barista. It's an interesting suggestion and one that sparked a long and lively debate.

We're delighted that George and Andrew's café has become a home from home for us all—great coffee, open air, a chance to meet both formally and informally. We're seeing a lot of laptops and cellphones on the tables down there. They are doing good business and we've been doing good business from their premises. It's a win—win.

But unfortunately, we can't agree to subsidize staff coffees there. We still have a significant number of employees who don't have either the time or inclination to go down to Mister Barista and so we need to maintain the coffee machines here at the office for their benefit. And that is where the coffee budget needs to go.

But given the huge volume of business we are sending to George and Andrew, we will try and secure a special discount from them over and above the loyalty card they currently offer.

No promises. But we'll do our best.

This is a memo that rejects a request. **But the top and tail format gives you the best chance of being positive while delivering this negative response.**

Q & A—To Clarify

The question and answer format is designed to show that you understand your reader's areas of concern. It enables you to identify and preempt any concerns that may yet develop. It also serves to explain and justify a course of action if you know your reader's specific criticisms.

Back to the Mister Barista saga—the board has decided to install expensive coffee machines. To cover the cost, they have decided to charge by the cup. The days of free bad coffee are over and the days of good coffee have arrived, but at a price. As office manager, you have to explain this decision.

To: All staff
From: You
Subject: **The new coffee machines**

From the start of next week, there will be new coffee machines on all floors. And for the first time, you will be charged $1 a cup. Some of you have asked me to explain this decision and I hope this memo will address your concerns.

Q: Why new machines?

A: We've had a torrent of complaints about the quality of the coffee and many staff felt that they were being forced to go to Mister Barista and pay $2 a cup. These new machines will deliver comparable quality at half the price.

Q: Why do we have to pay at all?

A: To cover the cost of the installation and the additional cost of supplying superior coffee.

Q: What if we don't want to pay? Does that mean no coffee?

A: There'll be instant coffee-making facilities in the kitchens. You'll find it slightly less disgusting than the stuff we used to dispense in the old machines. But you will have to bring your own cup and wash it up when you've finished.

Q: Why not use the money you are spending to subsidize cheaper coffee at Mister Barista?

A: The numbers don't work. We'd be running at a serious loss within nine months.

Any further questions, please don't hesitate to ask.

As with the Comparison structure, you have to play fair. People will quickly notice if you only ask yourself the easy questions. A better policy would be to make the questions as difficult for yourself as you can. Your credibility will go up.

The Diamond Structure—To Persuade

There are two versions of the Diamond Structure—one for simple and one for complex communications.

The simple structure is based on the Problem/Solution format we explored earlier but uses some of Aristotle's theories of rhetoric to make it more persuasive. Problem/Solution sets up your recommendation, and the Diamond format pushes it harder.

The complex version is based very closely on Aristotle's original schema.

He believed there are six stages in building a persuasive argument. They are:

1. The Introduction (Exordium). This is an overview of the situation that prepares the listener by establishing the scope of the discussion.

2. The Narrative (Narratio). This section explains what's happening and what brought us to this situation. It tells us the history.

3. The Partition (Divisio). This is a breakdown of the different topics that will be discussed.

4. The Confirmation (Confirmatio). These are the facts and arguments that support our case.

5. The Refutation (Confutatio). In this phase we preempt and refute any counter-arguments we can anticipate.

6. The Conclusion (Conclusio). This is where we summarize our arguments and deliver our recommendation in the form of a call to action.

When Aristotle developed his schema, he wasn't thinking about a businessman in front of a computer screen. His theories were intended for the face-to-face presentations and arguments that took place in the Athenian ecclesia, or citizens' assembly.

Nonetheless, his theories have endured as the core principles of persuasion and apply equally to the written and the spoken word.

Let's start with the simple structure.

Simple Diamond

The illustration at right shows the simple version of the Diamond.

You'll see it's made of three parts—a square with a triangle above and another below. **These three components are born of Aristotle's belief that all communication must have a beginning, a middle, and an end.**

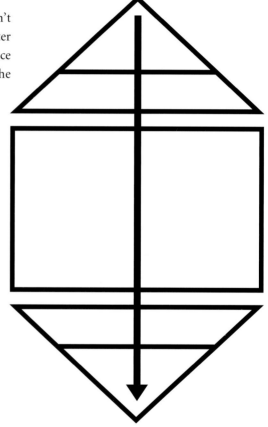

If you think of the Diamond as a flowchart, then the passage of time starts at the top and flows downward. The top triangle is where the communication starts and the subject is opened for discussion; the middle square is the largest section and forms the body and substance of your argument; the bottom triangle is where the communication is narrowed to a focus on your recommendation and then brought to an end.

These three sections are then further divided to reflect the subtleties of Aristotle's thinking. Let's look at each in turn. They are numbered in the illustration below.

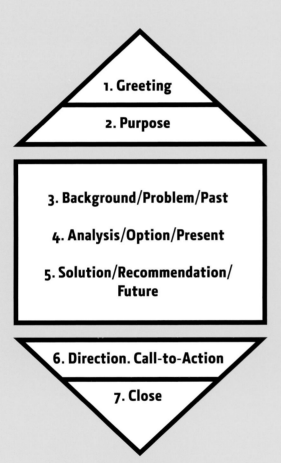

The Simple Diamond

1. Greeting
Apart from simple politeness, the intent of your greeting is to establish a connection and build a rapport.
You need to create a sense of togetherness between yourself and your reader if you are hoping that they are going to agree with what you have to say.

The style and content of the greeting will be influenced by the formality factor of the correspondence. Clearly, you'll adopt a very different tone if you are addressing someone you know well and who is likely to support you, than when you are writing to a stranger who is potentially hostile to your cause.

Use the greeting as an opportunity to set up your correspondence so that it relies more heavily on the words "you" and "we" and less on the word "I." (We'll look at how to create empathy in greater depth when we get to discuss language in Chapter 11.)

2. Purpose
These days, most people in business receive far more correspondence than they have time to read. So we tend to scan letters and emails to see if they are of any real interest. So state your purpose up front.

Tell your reader why you are writing. Let him or her know why this message is of value and why it should be treated with respect. Otherwise, you'll end up in the trash before you have made your first point.

3. Past—Background and/or Problem

Set the context of your request or recommendation by describing the problem and the events that created it. **Be descriptive and objective.** Keep your personal bias out of the communication at this point.

The purpose of this section is to bring you and the reader together "on the same page." If their interpretation of the past differs from yours, their expectations of the future will most likely be different and your recommendation will seem inappropriate. By the end of this section, you and the reader must agree on the nature of the problem and the events and forces that have created it.

> You may find that some of the other structures are useful within this section—Cause and Effect, Chronology, or Narrative.

4. Present—Analysis and Options

Once you have established the history, focus on the present. What are the effects of the problem and what options are available? What strategies are worth considering?

> You may find that the Comparison structure is useful in this section.

5. Future—Solution and Recommendation

Your recommendation must constitute a solution to the problem. After comparing options, concentrate on your proposal and explain what steps must be taken to make it happen.

> The Process structure often works well when making your recommendation.

6. Direction—Call to Action

Your recommendation is now on the table. You'll remember that, when considering your Purpose, you decided exactly what you wanted your reader to do. This is where you tell them. Leave them in no doubt. **Be specific about how you would like them to respond to your correspondence.**

> We've all received letters or emails that are full of interesting ideas, challenging observations, well-documented problems complete with possible solutions, and yet, at the end of the correspondence, we've found ourselves unsure of what to do next.
>
> That's a failed communication. Don't let it happen.

7. Close

As with your opening, the style of your closing will be decided by the formality of the correspondence. But formality does not affect the intent. The close is intended to leave your reader feeling positive. At the close of your message, your reader must feel a strong rapport with you. He or she must believe you understand the problem and have a viable solution.

Your reader must know exactly what you want them to think, feel, and do.

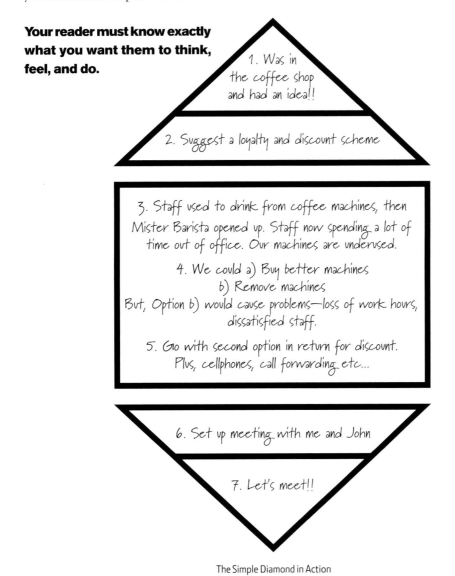

1. Was in the coffee shop and had an idea!!

2. Suggest a loyalty and discount scheme

3. Staff used to drink from coffee machines, then Mister Barista opened up. Staff now spending a lot of time out of office. Our machines are underused.

4. We could a) Buy better machines
   b) Remove machines
   But, Option b) would cause problems—loss of work hours, dissatisfied staff.

5. Go with second option in return for discount. Plus, cellphones, call forwarding etc...

6. Set up meeting with me and John

7. Let's meet!!

The Simple Diamond in Action

Let's look at an example of the Simple Diamond in action. Let's return to the unending saga of the coffee shop. This time you have been asked to write to the owners and start a negotiation for staff discounts. The illustration on the previous page shows you how the Simple Diamond might look when filled in, and here's an unpolished draft of the letter you might send:

Dear George and Andrew,

I was down at Mister Barista last week and delighted to see that your business is booming. In fact, it was after a particularly fine cup of your Colombian brew that I decided to write to you with this proposal.

I'd like to suggest that you consider a special loyalty deal for all of us who work here at the Gizmo Corporation.

Let me explain why.

Before you arrived, most of our staff drank coffee from the vending machines we provide at our offices. Not the greatest coffee to be sure, but inexpensive and better than nothing. (And, given the neighborhood back then, nothing was the alternative.)

Times have changed. Mister Barista now serves superb coffee, and so our vending machines are operating at about half their usual volume. And we've also noticed that our staff are spending more and more time out of the office.

As a consequence, the operating costs of our machines are unjustifiably high and we're losing person-hours while our employees are down at Mister Barista.

I can see two options:

We could invest in better machines and lure our staff back to their desks with a decent cup of coffee at a favorable price. But the initial investment would be high and there's no guarantee of success—some of our loyal staff are now your loyal customers!

Alternatively, we could remove our coffee machines and send all our business your way. But that would raise two issues. First, we'd lose even more person-hours. Second, about half of our staff would feel they are being forced to pay too much.

I think there is a solution.

My recommendation is that we go with the second option but, given the high volume of business our company would represent, we would need you to consider a substantial discount on coffee. (We wouldn't expect you to include food and pastries.) We can manage the empty desk problem by insisting our staff always carry their cellphones and use the call-forwarding service. We could even go so far as to supply some extra tables to allow the use of laptop computers.

If you are open to this proposal, the next step would be to meet with myself and John Brown, our finance director, to discuss terms and conditions.

Please call my assistant on 818-555-3456 to arrange a time that is convenient for you.

I'm sure we can come to an arrangement that works well for us all.

Let's do it over a decent cup of coffee!

Best regards,

You

This is not a polished letter. But the structure is sound. This ensures ease of understanding and leads the reader directly to your recommendation.

If you look back to Aristotle's schema, you'll see this Simple Diamond includes four of the six stages—only the Partition and Refutation are missing.

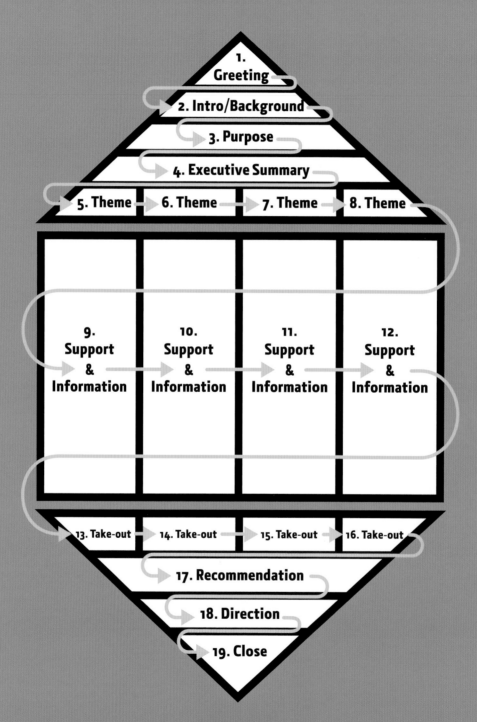

The Complex Diamond

Complex Diamond

In the Complex Diamond, we restore the Partition. This requires a change of structure, but provides two important benefits.

1. It allows us to introduce a more complex and detailed argument.
2. It allows us to reinforce our argument with the subtle use of repetition.

> The illustration on the opposite page shows the writing flow through the Complex Diamond. As with the simple version, the Complex Diamond has a beginning, middle, and end. Let's work through the individual sections.

1. Greeting

This serves exactly the same purpose as in the Simple Diamond. It needs to build a rapport with the reader or readers.

> If you are writing a complex document that will be read by a variety of recipients, you may not want to establish a personal tone. The greeting then needs to be a brief introduction to yourself and the subject.

2. Background

Give any relevant background information that explains the need for this particular communication.

3. Purpose

State the purpose of the communication. Why are you writing it? What benefits will the reader gain by reading it?

4. Executive Summary and Recommendation

If this is a long and complex document, a significant percentage of your readers will feel reluctant to wade through it. If they skim it, they might miss the point you are trying to make. Worse still, they might misunderstand the document and draw an entirely false conclusion.

> The best way to avoid this sort of miscommunication is to give them an Executive Summary up front.

An Executive Summary gives an overview of your main arguments and explains the recommendations you are going to make.
The summary must never be longer than a single page.

5–8. Themes

This is Aristotle's Partition. In sections 5 to 8 you outline the themes you are going to discuss. You don't explain or explore these themes, you simply say what they are.

In the case of Mister Barista, you might say your four themes are going to be:

A. Cost of providing free coffee versus cost of subsidizing an external supplier
B. Loss of working hours due to absenteeism
C. Options for creating an off-site working environment
D. Value of improved staff morale

The purpose of this is to prepare your reader's mind. You need them to allocate some neural pathways to the information you are going to send. This will lead to a subtle form of repetition as you are telling them what you are going to tell them. And the beauty of repetition, as long as it's not too obvious, is that it helps people to understand and remember what you are saying.

9–12. Content

Once you have established the themes of your argument you can explore each one in turn and deliver the content of your thoughts, information, and ideas. This is where you deliver the guts of your message. This is the body and substance of your communication.

Within these four stages, you can use any of the communication structures we discussed earlier: Problem/Solution, Cause/Effect, Chronology, and so on. Whatever gets the point across, use it.

13–16. Take-out

When you have made all of your points and delivered all of your arguments, don't imagine your readers will draw the same conclusions as you do yourself. They might choose an entirely different interpretation of the facts. This would be disastrous, so don't allow it. In sections 13–16, tell them exactly what you want them to take out of the arguments and information you have delivered. Give them the interpretation you want them to make.

If necessary, challenge all other interpretations. If there is a possible ambiguity, step on it now. In so doing, you are providing the last, missing piece of Aristotle's philosophy and strategy for persuasion—the Refutation.

17. Recommendation

You've given your readers the facts, you've told them how to interpret them. You're now ready to give them your recommendation. This will not come as a surprise. You have already given them an overview in the Executive Summary. But now you take them through the details of your recommendation.

18. Direction

Tell them exactly what you want them to do. If you have described a step-by-step process to achieve your goals, go back to the first step. Explain what they need to do after reading your communication. Help them take that first step.

19. Close

As with the Simple Diamond, end on a positive note. Be confident that your communication has brought you and your reader onto the same page. Anticipate taking the first step of your "Direction" together.

There's no rule that says you have to divide your content into four sections. The Diamond works just as well with three and could stretch to five—any more and you'd be stretching the concentration of your audience and you might want to consider condensing some of your material.

Ideally, you'll find the organization of your mind map fits comfortably with the structure of the Diamond. If you have four main branches radiating from your Purpose, they'll easily transfer to the themes, content, and take-outs of either a Complex or Simple Diamond. We've now looked at ten different formats. All of them are designed for specific communication tasks. We've finally reached the point where we are ready to write. In the next chapter we're going to see how our Preparation and Planning are going to make that an easy and enjoyable process.

Summary and Action points

1. There are 10 different formats we commonly use in business communication.
2. Each format serves a specific purpose.
3. The Organizational Diamond is specifically designed to make your writing more persuasive.
4. The other nine formats can be used within the structure of either the Simple or the Complex Diamond.

Exercise

You are George, proprietor of the Mister Barista coffee stand. You are writing to the Building Manager of the Gizmo Corporation to suggest a discount scheme and loyalty card for employees of the company.

You are offering only a 5% discount on coffee. It's less than expected.

Draw a Complex Diamond that shows how you would structure and justify your proposal.

9. The first draft

You may feel that it is taking an inordinately long time to reach the point where you actually start writing. But if you check your timeline, you'll see we have spent only about 40% of the time allowed for the project on Preparation and Planning.

That time has been well spent and will save you time in the next stages of the process.

What exactly have you achieved?

Preparation is the process in which you prepare your mind. This is what you did:

- You looked at how your communication style matches that of your readers
- You looked at how to get on their wavelength

Once you are used to doing this, it becomes intuitive and doesn't take very long at all.

Planning is the process in which you prepare your material. This is what you did:

- You established your purpose and desired outcome
- You developed a communication strategy
- You organized your information
- You chose a structure

Again, once you are familiar with this routine, it doesn't take very long. But it does mean that when you do start writing, you know exactly what you are going to say—you have a clear intent, the right information in the right place, and a structure that will add power to your delivery.

What may surprise you is that much of the writing has already taken place in your head without your even noticing. All you have to do now is get it on the page.

Free-flow Writing

Psychology professor and author Mihaly Csikszentmihalyi describes a state of mind where we become totally and happily absorbed in a task. He calls this experience "Flow." It occurs, he believes, when our competence is perfectly matched to a challenge we have undertaken.

You are now ready to get into Flow. The challenge you face is to write a piece of persuasive communication. Your planning and preparation will ensure that you have all the necessary competence to meet that challenge and become deeply absorbed in the process.

Here's what you do: take a blank sheet of paper and start writing. And don't stop. Or open a new blank document on your word processor and start typing.

That's it. Very simple. Start writing and keep writing until you have finished your first draft.

When I say, "Don't stop," I mean exactly that. Don't re-read anything you have written. Don't correct any mistakes you may think you have made. Just keep going. Let the words pour out of you. If you temporarily dry up, write anything that keeps your pen moving or the keyboard clattering. Write, "I can't think of what to write, I can't think of what to write, I'm an idiot, help, help, etc., etc." (I'm not suggesting you write these words. That's just the sort of junk I write when I hit a dry spot.)

Eventually, your mind will re-engage with your subject and the words will start to flow again. Perfectionists will find this hard at first. They like to get every sentence just right. Then they want every paragraph to be just right. They move backward and forward constantly correcting and rewriting or starting again. Their progress is painfully slow.

> The way to escape this psychological trap is to believe and remember that your first draft is merely the raw material of your communication. No one is going to read it with the exception of yourself. There is no need to feel self-conscious. There is no need for it to be perfect.

But there is a very real need for you to let your subconscious have its say. There's a lot going on down there. While you have been consciously preparing and planning, the deeper levels of your mind have been processing information and putting things together. It's time to set these thoughts free. So get out of the way!

> Suspend all self-judgment and self-consciousness, and let it all out. After all, if you don't like it you can change it, and no one will know.

However, it's more likely that you'll be surprised.

> Most of the participants in the workshops we run are amazed to find that, with the right preparation and planning, writing becomes an effortless, almost automatic process. Flow is liberating. It feels great. The agonies of indecision and doubt are forgotten. All worries about the assignment and the end result are replaced by a total absorption in the moment—and the moment is all about watching the words appear on the page. We observe the process rather than control it. We just allow it to happen. Sometimes it can feel that the words are flowing through us and not from us—in Flow, we become a conduit.

Don't stop until you have exhausted your thoughts and feel that you have covered your subject.

If you have a tendency to keep checking spelling or formatting your work while you write, try using the Drafting tool that is on the CD that came with this book. It's a primitive word processor and timer. It's easy to use. It lets you write in ten-minute blocks and has most functions disabled. It just lets you write—no reviewing, no grammar correction, no paragraphs. By removing these unnecessary distractions, you can concentrate on getting the raw material on the page. Tidying it all up comes later.

Writer's Block

But what if you get stuck? Really stuck.

In my experience, writer's block comes from two things:

- **Poor preparation**
- **Nerves and fear**

You can't expect the right words and thoughts to appear if you haven't prepared well. That is why the first 40% of the process is so important. But if that is the problem, it's an easy fix. Go back and do your groundwork.

Fear is a more insidious problem. What exactly do we fear? Failure, embarrassment, criticism, rejection—all the old favorites. The process of writing externalizes some of our innermost thoughts and puts them on display. We feel vulnerable.

Some years ago, I was in a writing class in London and the tutor showed us a devious technique for defeating writer's block. His belief was that the little voice inside our heads, our inner critic, is entirely to blame for the problem. We try to write, and, instead of hearing the words we need to transcribe, we hear a destructive criticism and running commentary along the lines of: "This isn't very good," "You can't write, this sounds wrong," "People are going to read this and think it's garbage!" and so on.

His suggestion was that, when writing, keep a small pad of notepaper within reach. When you hear your little voice start to needle you and undermine your confidence, write down what it is saying on that pad. Write down, "You're a failure. You can't write to save your life!" or whatever mean-spirited critique you are struggling to endure while trying to write. His theory, which works for me, is that by externalizing these self-inflicted wounds, we can rid ourselves of them. Basically, get them out of your head so that you can get on with the job. From time to time, when you have filled a page of the note pad, crumple it up and throw it in the garbage. It's a gesture of self-affirmation and defiance of your fears. Sounds silly perhaps, but I've found it clears my head.

Using Dictation

Another technique for engaging the mind and getting your words to flow is to talk instead of write. But for this to work you need to be able to talk at a reasonable speed and record what it is that you are saying. (It's very frustrating to say something coherent out loud and then find you have forgotten it when you try and type it onto the page.)

It seems unlikely that you'll have a secretary on hand who can take dictation at the speed you can blather. But, thanks to the miracle of digital technology, that is no longer necessary. There are now several software packages for both the Mac and PC that will transcribe your spoken words directly into your favorite word-processing program.

It takes an hour or so to set up one of these systems, as your computer has to learn to recognize your words in spite of any accent you may have. But once it can "hear" you correctly, these systems are surprisingly fast and accurate. (And surprisingly inexpensive.)

If you have prepared well and have your structure written out in front of you, then it's quite easy to dictate your message without rambling or getting off the point.

The writing part of the assignment then becomes the cleaning up and polishing, which we'll be studying later.

Taking a Break

When you've finished your first draft, don't immediately re-read it and start hacking into it. Leave it. Take a break.

The best way to disengage your mind from what you have been doing is to do something else. Have a cup of coffee or tea, or go for a walk. Talk to someone. Or read something that is not connected to the subject on which you have been writing. It only takes a few minutes to get out of your writer's mindset to prepare yourself for a new role—reader. When you review your work, you must temporarily cease to be you and become the person to whom you are writing.

Reading

One simple trick for switching perspectives is to change the medium. If you have been typing on a computer, then print out your draft. Before you do, change the typeface to one you would never normally use. Change its size too. Make it bigger or smaller than your default setting.

If you have been writing by hand, photocopy it, and change the size slightly. Ideally, when you read your draft you want to feel as if you are seeing it for the first time. The more unfamiliar it feels, the more objective you will be when you evaluate it.

Before you read, refer back to your notes on the audience profile. What communication and writing preferences do they have? Are they fact-loving Blues or process-driven Greens? Are they emotionally charged Reds or do they display the creativity and curiosity of the Yellows? Try to occupy their headspace before you read.

Then read it through once and get the feel of the thing. Sometimes it helps to read it out loud and see where you are trying to put the emphasis.

Then read it a second time and make notes of any obvious omissions or elements that feel wrong and should be deleted.

You're now ready to rewrite it.

Summary and Action points

1. Review the notes you made during Preparation and Planning.

2. Write a first draft without stopping. Don't re-read, correct, or change anything. Keep writing for at least ten minutes. Write as quickly as you can, keep moving the pen or hammering the keyboard.

3. If you do stop, write something, anything.

4. Take a break and disengage. Do something else for ten minutes.

5. Change the medium—either print or photocopy your draft.

6. Become your reader, see your words through their eyes and preferences.

7. Read aloud and get a sense of where you are trying to place your emphasis.

8. Get the feel of it.

9. Make a note of anything that should be removed or added.

Exercise

1. Write for ten minutes, without stopping, on one of the following subjects:

   - Your first day at school
   - The interview for your first job
   - Waking up on Christmas morning
   - Finding a spider on your pillow

Don't worry about structure, get into Flow and go with it. You'll surprise yourself!

2. Take the draft that you just wrote and read it through the eyes of someone who has communication preferences diametrically opposed to your own. See what changes you would need to make to get on to their wavelength.

10. The second draft– strengthening your content

You now have a crude version or model of your letter on the page. Thanks to the Planning and Preparation you did at the outset, the structure should be sound—the right information in the right place. But before you start honing and polishing it, you need to be sure that nothing is missing. The second draft is still concerned with content and focuses on Opening, Closing, the Body of Information, and Techniques of Persuasion.

The Opening

Let's start at the start. Your opening needs to achieve the following four goals:

- Grab and hold the reader's attention
- Explain why you are writing
- Reveal the structure of your communication
- Set the tone of the correspondence

Grabbing Attention

Recently, I received a letter from a firm of Executive Search Consultants who wanted to explain some career opportunities to a fugitive from the advertising industry. Me. Their letter started with these words:

Dear Nick,

Headhunters International [not their real name] has been established in Sydney for more than ten years and, thanks to our local and overseas experience, we are uniquely positioned to give advice on executive career development in marketing and advertising.

There's nothing untruthful about this first paragraph but there's nothing very interesting about it either. I suspect they wrote to me because an industry magazine had recently published the ages of the creative directors working in the city and they had noticed that I was in the upper level. I'll never know because I never replied to their letter.

There are five simple tactics they could have used to make my eyes widen a little and get me involved—a fact, a question, a challenge, a story, or a request.

Dear Nick,

By the age of 55, more than 95% of creative directors have left the agency side of the advertising business. But that doesn't mean they have stopped being creative.
Headhunters International…

This fact would have held my attention to the point where they could make some sort of proposal.

Dear Nick,

Have you ever wondered what most creative directors do when they finally decide to leave the agency business? Have you already made plans for what your next career is going to be?

Headhunters International…

By asking a question that touches a nerve, they would have secured my rapt attention. I'd have read every word they had to say.

Dear Nick,

Name three creative directors who have quit advertising and gone on to have successful careers outside the agency business.

At Headhunters International we can name many more than three…

A challenge is a powerful technique for gaining involvement. A challenge creates an immediate interaction. The reader has to respond even if it's only in his or her own mind.

Dear Nick,

When John Smith left BDM after seven years as creative director, he really wasn't sure where the future was going to take him. But after more than 20 years of winning awards, he wasn't ready to throw in the creative towel.

So he came to see us at Headhunters International. We…

A story that relates to my own experience is one I'm going to read. We love to know how other people handle the challenges we face. It's the next best thing to reading about ourselves!

Dear Nick,

We'd like to meet you and talk to you about what you plan to do when you decide to leave the agency business behind.

As you may know, by the age of 55 most creative directors….

Sometimes, a simple request is the most immediate way to engage your reader's attention. If the request is clearly relevant to their situation and needs, it will mean you are relevant to them. They'll read on.

I'm not saying that every communication must follow the formula of starting with one of these devices. But I am saying that every communication must start by establishing a rapport with the reader. Within a few lines, you must establish some form of commonality—common ground, common aspirations or needs, common values. The opening must break down the invisible barrier between writer and reader and replace it with a sense of shared interest.

Explain Yourself

Once you have your reader's attention, you must quickly explain why you are writing. What's the purpose of this communication? The Diamond structure forces you to do this. Get the hook in and then tell the reader what they are going to get in return for their time and attention.

> In the case of my letter from the Executive Search Agency, they started off talking about themselves. Then they talked about their ability to shape careers within advertising and marketing. But what I needed to hear was that they also helped build second careers. I was interested in life after advertising. Unfortunately, that came at the end of their letter. (Lucky I was still reading!)

Reveal the Structure of Your Communication

Your planning and structure have given you a map of where your communication is going. You know the destination and the route to it. But your reader is clueless. So help them. Give them some signposts that will help them stay the course.

> Again, the Organizational Diamond forces you to do this. After establishing your purpose it exposes the themes of your correspondence before getting into the details.

If you are writing to someone who is likely to skim your letter, this bird's-eye view will help them find the information they need. In other words, they'll skim it more effectively and, we hope, be sufficiently engaged to go back and read it thoroughly.

Set the Tone

In your opening lines you must clearly establish the tone and mood of your letter.

Your salutation must reflect the level of formality you chose during the Planning stage. Email seems to have multiplied the number of different options. New ones are "Hi," "Hello," or no salutation at all. The old standbys are still available: "Dear Sir," "Dear Mr. or Ms. Surname," "Dear First Name," and even the utterly impersonal "To whom it may concern."

It's a judgment call and the easy way to make it is to imagine you are reading the letter aloud to your intended recipient. Imagine they've lost their glasses and have asked you to read it to them. You'll immediately get a feeling for what is appropriate.

As far as tone goes, the rule is simple. Be positive. Even if you are delivering bad news or discussing a serious problem, a positive tone of voice is more engaging. Negativity just switches people off.

Once you are happy that the opening is working for you, forget the body of your letter and head straight for the end.

The Closing

The opening and closing must work together. These will be the most memorable elements of your communication—the words that engaged the reader's attention at the start and the instructions or call to action at the very end.

In the opening, you established a destination and set a course to take the reader there. In the closing, you will need to do two things:

1. Reassure the reader that you have delivered on your promise and taken them to the right place. So remind them of that opening promise.

2. Give them instructions that explain specifically what you want them to do next. Make sure they understand your desired outcome.

The Organizational Diamond will create the necessary symmetry between the start and the finish of your letter. But there is an important distinction to make between a letter that issues an order and one that intends to persuade.

If you are in a position to command a certain response, then you can close with a definitive call to action. But if you are trying to persuade your reader to act in the way you'd like, then you'll need to leave a door open for further communication.

An order assumes compliance—it's a one-way communication unless your authority is challenged. But when you seek to influence or persuade someone to comply with a request, it's a two-way communication. You'll need the reassurance of hearing their consent and so you must close in a way that encourages them to reply.

If you don't, you risk a communication breakdown or an impasse in which nothing happens.

The Body of Information

When you are happy that the beginning and end are working in tandem, you can concentrate on making the body strong. You need to look at four things—specificity, examples, proof, and visual support.

Be Specific and Use Examples

The body of your text is where you will place most of the information that supports your point of view. There's a simple principle you must apply: general information is weak, specific information is strong.

Whenever possible, support every statement you make with facts and statistics. Illustrate your points with examples.

Compare the following: In recent months we've seen a dramatic decrease in the number of applications.

With: Since February we have seen a dramatic 30% decrease in the number of applications.

Or: We're doing everything we can to protect our current consumer base.

With: We've introduced a new price structure and loyalty card scheme to protect our current consumer base.

Or: If we fail to secure the government contract the consequences will be dire.

With: If we fail to secure the government contract, we'll lose credibility with our major suppliers (AMCO and Simlex) and be forced to reduce staff by up to 25%.

Sweeping statements that are loaded with adjectives, adverbs, and strong language may seem powerful, but they're not. We may think in ideas, but we remember ideas by the facts that support them. Always try to convert the abstract into the real.

If you want to be convincing, then support everything you say with a fact, a statistic, or an example. If you can't find one, you must challenge the value of what you are trying to communicate. Maybe you should be saying something more robust.

Use Proof to Create Belief

In the battle between opinion and objective truth, truth usually wins. (I wish I could say it always wins.) So the question is, how do we give our opinion the value and power of truth? The answer is we need proof. A motto to remember:

Saying it is so doesn't make it so.

Your reader may have a profound respect for everything you say and you may express yourself in the most convincing manner but, if the evidence contradicts you, your views will eventually be discredited and disregarded. (Ask Bill Clinton.)

When reviewing the body of your letter, check every assertion you make and find a way of substantiating it. Find credible evidence that supports you.

This could come in the form of verifiable facts and figures, the testimony of experts and witnesses, case studies, real-life examples, or images. Imagine you are in a court of law and you must prove your case "beyond a reasonable doubt." Always think of your reader as a skeptic who must be convinced.

Use Visuals to Explain and Support

Some information is better explained through imagery. Fortunately, we have developed a visual language to do this. Pie charts give an immediate impression of how the totality of something is divided. Bar graphs allow us to make comparative rankings. Graphs display data relative to fluctuations, trends, and time-related events. A quadrant matrix is effective in showing how two variables can interact. Photographs give documentary evidence, and diagrams can show the internal workings of a hidden mechanism.

For example, if I were to say to you that your portfolio contained investments that were 20% in managed funds, 29% in overseas investments, 13% in domestic property and 38% in commercial property, would you understand and remember this information as easily as if I showed you this chart?

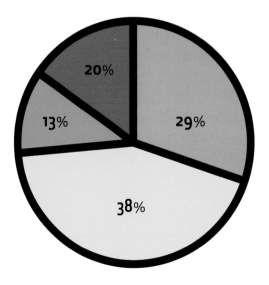

Probably not.

Don't be afraid to use visuals to strengthen your case. With the advent of Google Images, I think we'll see a trend of using more visual information in written communication, as it is becoming so accessible.

The Powers of Persuasion

Lastly, to complete our second draft and ensure we have the appropriate content, we should see if Robert Cialdini's Weapons of Influence can be of any help in strengthening our argument or message.

Cialdini worked with many different sales organizations to understand how they developed their powers of influence and persuasion. His conclusion is that there are six weapons or principles:

They are:

The Principle of Liking

The Principle of Reciprocity

The Principle of Consistency

The Principle of Social Proof

The Principle of Authority

The Principle of Scarcity

Let's take them one at a time.

The Principle of Liking is simply that people feel predisposed toward those whom they perceive as liking them. In other words, we like to be liked. To apply this principle to written communication we need to uncover similarities between ourselves and our readers and, when possible, be positive about their involvement in any issue we are discussing.

The Principle of Reciprocity is that people "repay in kind." In business this means we should give what we hope to receive. That may be advice, information, help, support, or service of one sort or another.

The Principle of Consistency is that people "align with their commitments." Reminding people of a verbal or written commitment is one way of ensuring they stick to it.

The Principle of Social Proof is that "people follow the lead of similar others." This is a powerful tool in persuasion. If you can show testimonials and references that support your recommendations from people in the reader's peer group, you will strengthen your case considerably.

The Principle of Authority is that people "defer to experts." If you have expertise, don't hide it. Don't assume it's self-evident and don't give in to modesty. Your expertise is a strong endorsement of your point of view.

The Principle of Scarcity is based on the notion that "people want more of what they can have less of." Wherever it is appropriate and ethical, exclusive offers are very powerful. An opportunity becomes more attractive if it is unique.

Review these six weapons or principles when completing your second draft. See if any of them can increase the persuasion quotient of your message. Once that process is complete, you can relax in the knowledge that you now have the right content in the right place. Your structure is sound.

You are ready to start polishing.

Summary and Action points

1. Review the opening. Ensure you engage the reader, explain your purpose, establish the structure of your correspondence, and set the appropriate tone.

2. Review the closing. Reiterate your promise and clearly state your call to action.

3. Review the body of information. Ensure you are specific, use examples, substantiate all claims with proof, and illustrate with imagery if necessary.

4. Review the Six Weapons of Influence and see if you can use any of them to strengthen your powers of persuasion if necessary.

Exercise

Rummage through your files or the "Sent Items" folder on your email application and find a lengthy piece of communication you have sent—at least 200 words.

Re-edit it using the process described in this chapter.

11. Adjusting style and language

I used to work with a typographer in advertising who had a poster on his office wall that read: "You can't polish a turd!"

Every day people brought him half-baked ideas and expected him to make their work look good. His poster was intended to scare them off by sending this simple message: if the structure and content of something is not right, no amount of polishing is going to make it shine.

His philosophy holds true for writing. Everything we have done so far has been to ensure we have the right information in a format that makes sense of it. Now that is done, we are ready to start buffing it up.

Each of the exercises in this chapter is short, easy, and effective. It's no more difficult than wiping a rag over a tarnished metal surface. But the result makes a world of difference. The more you polish, the brighter it gleams. And the brighter it gleams, the more people take notice of it.

The Empathy Factor

It's important that your reader, and not you, is the focus of the communication. If you want to engage the audience, talk directly to them and about them.

> When polishing, this is an easy fix. You need to establish the Empathy Factor of your text by counting the number of references to your reader and subtracting the number of references to yourself. Ideally, you'll end up with a positive number. This means your correspondence is reader-focused. (Ignore any joint references to reader and writer—usually in the form of "we.")

Let's look at a sample paragraph. It's a claim that could be made by a photo-processing laboratory:

> Q-Snap has installed the latest digital technology so that we can provide state-of-the-art prints in less than one hour.

I've underlined the references to the writer. There are no references to the reader. Therefore, 0 - 2 = -2. The Empathy Factor is -2. Not too good.

Let's try again.

You'll get state-of-the-art prints and you'll wait less than an hour thanks to the latest digital technology at Q-Snap.

> In the rewrite we have two references to the reader and one to the writer: 2 - 1 = +1. This sentence now has a positive empathy factor. It's reader-focused.

> When polishing your second draft, check the Empathy Factor of the document and make sure you raise it to a positive number. Take any opportunity to use the pronouns "You" and "Your" or, without getting excessive, use your reader's name.

Try to create the sense of a personal relationship even within the most formal correspondence. That doesn't mean you should become overly familiar. It means you should find areas of shared interest and concern so that your reader feels connected to you.

> The spirit of your letter should be "we"— you and the reader together.

Clear Writing

Languages are alive. New words, especially technical words, are being added all the time, and hot phrases and jargon come and go. This should mean that we are able to express ourselves more clearly and precisely. Unfortunately, that's not always the case.

We choose words that we think will make us look better. We imagine that longer, more obscure words suggest intellectual sophistication that people will find impressive.

A great deal of business writing is confused by this prejudice. The fact remains that shorter words are easier to read and obscure words are harder to understand.

So keep it plain and simple. Avoid the pretentious, convoluted business speak that renders so many letters unintelligible. And remember, clarity is the most impressive quality in business writing. Clear writing suggests a clear mind and a clear understanding of the issues.

Subject your draft to the following criteria: **Short, Simple, Strong, Smooth.**

Short

Look for opportunities in the draft to shorten every word, phrase, and paragraph.

First, look for words that can be deleted. You'll find subtle tautologies if you look hard enough. Words are cheap. Don't be afraid to throw them away.

Here are some examples:
We might possibly extend the contract for a period of two years.

What use are the words "possibly" and "a period of"?

We might extend the contract for two years.

That's shorter and sharper.

Here's another one:
The problem arose at a time when we least expected it.

Why use "at a time?"

The problem arose when we least expected it.

Read your draft very carefully and delete every word that isn't needed. Be ruthless.

Then move on to phrases.

It's surprising how many verbs have, quite unnecessarily, expanded into phrases. Here are just five examples.

Agree	**Reach an agreement**
Explain	**Give an explanation**
Adjust	**Make an adjustment**
Meet	**Hold a meeting**
Conclude	**Bring to a conclusion**

Weed them out. When a single word can replace a phrase without loss of meaning, make the substitution.

Then move onto paragraphs.

The rule for paragraphs is simple. The first sentence introduces the point you are going to make. Every subsequent sentence relates to it. When the point is made, move onto the next paragraph.

The problem occurs when you have too much support information and the paragraph becomes long and feels drawn out. We need to do one of two things:

- **Enumerate the points you are making within the paragraph**
- **Use bullet points to break the paragraph up**

For example:

Dear John,
I found your letter frustrating. First, you didn't explain your purpose in writing to me. Second, I found the information confusing and disorganized. Third, the language was technical and verbose. And last, by the end of it I was unsure what you wanted me to do.
I suggest you buy a book on business writing.

Or

> *Dear John,*
> *I found your letter frustrating for four reasons:*
> - *I didn't know why you were writing in the first place.*
> - *The information was confusing and disorganized.*
> - *The language was technical and verbose.*
> - *It gave me no clear direction.*
> *I suggest you buy a book on business writing.*

Either of these techniques will make the paragraph easier to read and remember.

Always avoid paragraphs that run to ten or more sentences. They look "heavy" on the page and are uninviting. Find a way of subdividing them. In business writing, the Bauhaus philosophy of "less is more" works very well. It saves the reader's time and effort and they will appreciate you for that.

Simple

Your readers must never find themselves asking, "I wonder what that means exactly?"

Don't try to impress them by displaying your ability to use obscure language or jargon. You'll only frustrate them. Jargon can usually be replaced by words in plain English. And if you have to use an acronym, give the full definition in parentheses after the first time it appears in the text. Don't assume your reader knows its meaning.

Simple is best. Don't say, "Activate," say "Start." Don't say, "Concur," say "Agree." And so on. Try to use language that would feel comfortable in conversation. But above all, avoid clichés. If words are cheap, clichés are cheaper and always sound stale. Avoid this sort of thing:

1. The bottom line
2. Rocket science
3. A ballpark figure
4. At the end of the day
5. The big picture
6. The level playing field
7. Pushing the envelope
8. Between a rock and a hard place

There are thousands of clichés, all of them cringeworthy. Don't use them. Instead, try to strip any clichéd business talk out of your writing:

Dear John,
    Pursuant to our conversation of July 10, please find the enclosed documents pertaining to the contract amendments.

People actually write like this when all they really need to say is:

Dear John,
    As discussed on July 10, I'm enclosing the documents explaining the changes to the contract.

Ironically, it's easier to write in simple, conversational language. Just forget any idea whose convoluted phrasing sounds more appropriate for business.

Strong

You can add strength and conviction to your writing by using an active tone of voice. Passive writing feels vague and weak.

This is best explained with some examples:
The books were ordered by us on the 18th.
Versus: We ordered the books on the 18th.

The first is passive while the second is active and sounds more positive and dynamic.

Similarly: A decision was made by the board to cancel the contract.
Versus: The board decided to cancel the contract.

It's a question of emphasis and deciding who or what is the true subject of your sentence. In this last example, clearly the board and not the decision is the subject, and the structure of the sentence should make that clear. The discipline of focusing on the subject will also affect where you place nouns and verbs.
For example: It's going to be difficult to change the deadline.
This statement can be made more dynamic by establishing the focus.
Changing the deadline will be difficult.

Or: The deadline will be difficult to change.

Or: The difficulty will be in changing the deadline.

In this example, there are three options for emphasis—difficulty, change, or deadline. Decide on the focus of your attention and then build the sentence around it.

On the other hand, there may be occasions when, for diplomacy or to avoid responsibility, you deliberately choose the passive mode:

Mistakes have been made.

Versus: We made mistakes. **Or:** You made mistakes.

Either way, be conscious of the subject and then compose the sentence to make your emphasis clear.

You can also add some muscle to your writing by choosing powerful verbs and nouns instead of overloading your sentences with adjectives and adverbs.

Compare these two sentences:

It's very important that we get the contract signed as quickly as possible.

It's imperative that the contract is signed now.

Keep an eye out for the word "very." We often use it to make a weak adjective or adverb sound stronger. A better approach is to find a stronger word.

Describe a big house as a "mansion," or running fast as "sprinting." Look for words that are strong enough not to need the support of modifiers.

Also, be wary of words and phrases that sound meaningful but are redundant.

Avoid these, for example:

In this day and age

At this point in time

All in all

Really

It's a fact that

In today's society

There are many such phrases and they creep into our writing when we are trying to sound relaxed and informal. Unfortunately, we end up sounding sloppy.

Also, be alert for redundancy or repetition.

> The plane landed at the airport in the early hours of the morning.
>
> **Versus:** The plane landed early in the morning.

> Unless this is a report of an aviation disaster, we can assume it landed at an airport. The word "hours" adds nothing to our understanding of time.

Lastly, you can make your writing stronger by using a positive tone of voice. People shy away from negatives.

Consider the difference between these two sentences:

> Absolutely no children admitted without an adult.
>
> **Versus:** Children welcome when accompanied by an adult.

The meaning is the same. But one expresses a negative while implying a positive and the other expresses a positive while implying a negative. The positive expression is less likely to provoke reader resistance.

> **Similarly:** We cannot process applications received after June 10.
>
> **is less engaging than:** Please return all applications before the June 10 deadline.

Smooth

> Once your draft is short, simple, and strong then you must work on its flow. It needs to be smooth.

Your writing takes your reader on a journey—from opening hook to final conclusion. And while there may be changes of pace, you must avoid any distracting bumps, sudden lurches, or swerves in direction. Each sentence must lead directly to the next. Each paragraph must emerge from the one that precedes it. If your writing lacks continuity, you risk losing your reader's attention as they try to piece your thoughts together. That's your job, not theirs.

Continuity comes from two things:

- **Structure**
- **Language**

If you have structured your information carefully—the Organizational Diamond guarantees this—then getting from one point to the next will be easy. The structure will provide a path for your reader to follow.

Language, the link words you choose, will then provide the stepping stones along that path and make it easy to follow.

Accuracy

When your draft reads well and is written clearly—when it's short, simple, strong, and smooth—then the real writing is done. All that remains is to check for accuracy.

We need to check factual content. And we need to check spelling and grammar.

Content

This is a simple process:

- Verify all figures. If necessary cite the source.
- Check quotes for accuracy and name the speaker.
- Give references for any research findings.

When polishing your draft, bear any personal bias in mind and, looking through your reader's eyes, try to see if you have understated or overstated your case. And then adjust it if necessary.

Spelling and Grammar

If you are using a word processor, spelling is not too much of an issue. Just run the spell-checker and make the necessary corrections. Make sure you have the right dictionary loaded. As I write for you now, a lot of words are underlined in red because I use an American version of Microsoft Word and I write with English spellings. This book will be published in multiple languages, so someone will have to produce two versions of this manuscript and I assume they'll just load a different dictionary and check it again.

But be warned. A spell-checker only finds words that are spelled incorrectly and therefore don't exist. If you write "you" instead of "your," the software won't pick it up because the dictionary contains the word "you." Spell-checkers are not context- or meaning-sensitive. So check the easy words yourself.

If you are writing by hand, you'll have a similar problem. You'll notice the difficult words—they leap off the page at you. But the simple, easy words are the ones you may overlook.

Be diligent. A spelling mistake is a small thing. But some readers attach a lot of importance to it. They see it as sloppiness or indifference and that becomes a comment on you and not just on your writing.

> Be especially careful with names. If you want to get on the wrong side of someone, spell their name incorrectly! You immediately establish yourself as a stranger.

Lastly, grammar. Language is constantly evolving but the rules change very slowly. We just break them more and it becomes increasingly acceptable to do so. We end sentences with prepositions and we start them with "And." We sometimes split infinitives, and so on.

> But as the poet, playwright, and critic T. S. Eliot said, "It's not wise to violate the rules until you know how to observe them."

> Most good business writing has a conversational tone and a slight bending of the rules is perfectly permissible. But if your correspondence is particularly formal, you'd be advised to obey the law.

This book is not a reference book for English syntax and grammar. But there are many such books. *Rules of Thumb for Business Writers* by Roberts, Hughes, and Silverman is packed with excellent tips and advice that will help you follow the rules of correct English. If you are writing by hand, such a reference book will prove extremely useful.

> However, if you are using a word processor, you'll find most of the assistance you need within the software. Microsoft Word comes with comprehensive spelling- and grammar-checking facilities, and you should always make use of them before sending out a document. You'll be surprised at how often it will pick up simple errors in documents that you've already read through a number of times!

Proofreading

Your third and polished draft has been subjected to very thorough testing and revision. It should be perfect. But every now and then, something will slip through the net. Proofreading is your last chance to make sure that an important document does not contain any errors.

The more familiar you are with the text, the harder it is to spot the mistakes. So one option is to get someone else to do it. They'll look at it with fresh eyes and see problems that have become invisible to you. It's also the easiest way of getting the job done.

But if the task falls to you alone, here are some tips.

- Read the text aloud. This will alert you to any problems with flow.
- Change the medium. If you've been working on a computer screen, print the text and proofread the page.
- Read the text out of order. Start with the last sentence and work backward. This will stop you jumping over words because you can anticipate them.
- Slow down by running your finger under the words as you read. (Don't do this in the office in front of your colleagues.) Or use a pencil or ruler under the line you are reading to mask the line below and stop you skipping ahead.
- Search for one problem at a time—spelling, punctuation, capital letters, and so on.
- Take a break and then check it one last time.

Summary and Action points

1. Calculate the empathy factor of your document by subtracting the number of references to yourself from the number of references to your reader. Ensure you have a positive figure.
2. Translate your words into plain English by applying the 4 S-words: Short, Simple, Strong, Smooth.
3. Check for accuracy in Content, Spelling, and Grammar.
4. Proofread the finished document.

Exercise

Take your edited text from the exercise at the end of Chapter 12 and polish it by following the processes in this chapter.

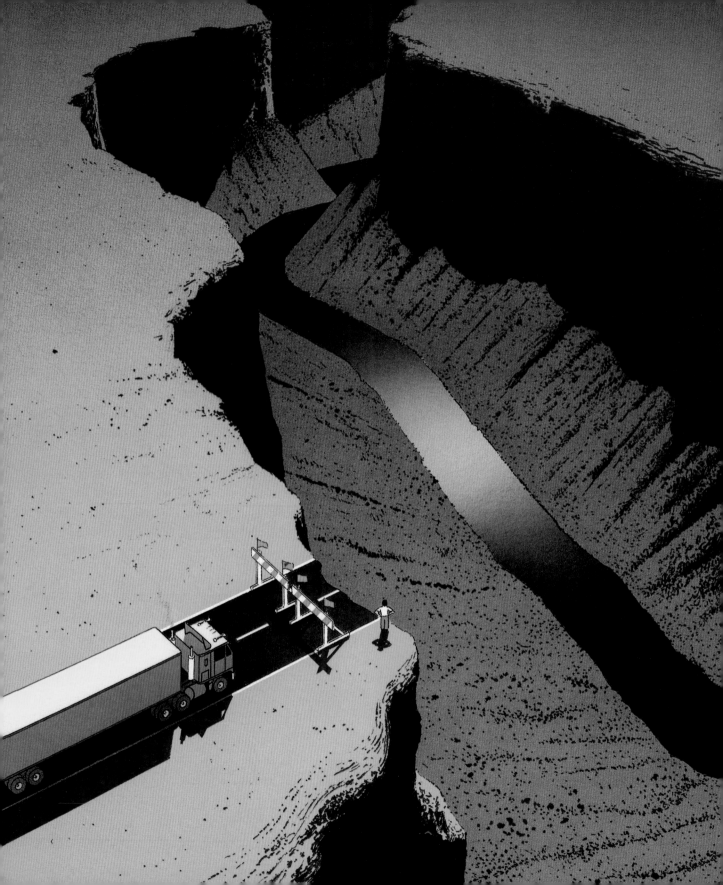

12. Conclusion

From start to finish we've worked through six stages:

It sounds like a drawn-out process, but it's not. In fact, it will save you time. You'll also get a better result. And that will save you more time—a well-written letter or email can stop the ping-pong effect of sending and receiving more and more letters that don't nail the issue.

- **Preparation**
- **Planning**
- **Drafting**
- **Reviewing**
- **Rewriting**
- **Polishing**

So, in conclusion, let's establish a checklist that will take you quickly through the process.

Before you start, decide how long you can allow for the assignment and use the timeline to establish the number of minutes you can dedicate to each stage.

1. Purpose

Understand the purpose of your communication and know exactly what you want your reader to do once they have read it.

2. Understand Your Reader, Understand Yourself

Remember the 4 Ps:

Personality, Prejudice, Pressures, Position

Try to identify your reader's communication preferences. Are they Blue and want facts, are they Green and want process, are they Red and want emotion, or are they Yellow and want conceptual thinking?

Understand what prejudices you may have to overcome before your reader is receptive to your message.

Find out what pressures are being exerted on your reader by the formal and hidden cultures in which he or she is working.

Try to identify where your reader is in the Stages of Change.

Finally, consider how you relate to your reader and decide how you may have to adjust your style so that your content and tone of voice is appropriate.

3. Develop a Communication Strategy

- **Establish the nature of the task using the matrix shown in the Challenge Matrix in Chapter 6**
- **Identify any obstacles and barriers**
- **Build a frame for your argument**
- **Determine the level of formality**
- **Choose the appropriate medium**
- **Set the tone of the communication**

4. Gather Your Information

Use mind mapping to explore everything you know about the subject. Then use WIIFM? to turn claims into values and benefits that you can prove.

5. Choose a Structure

There are ten common structures but if your intention is to be persuasive, use the Organizational Diamond.

6. Write a First Draft

Get into Flow mode and write a first draft without stopping or revising. Don't re-read, just write until you reach the end.

7. Review

Change your point of view and review your first draft as if seeing it through your reader's eyes.

8. Write a Second Draft

Concentrate on content. Start with the opening and make sure it is powerful, engaging, and clearly states your intentions.

Then move onto the conclusion and make sure it works in tandem with the opening and clearly states your call to action.

Then strengthen your body of information by being specific, adding examples, proof, and, if necessary, visual support.

Re-read this draft and see if the Six Weapons of Influence can be used to make your content more persuasive.

9. Write Your Final Draft

Polish your writing. Start by raising the Empathy Factor. Then translate your words into plain English by applying the 4 S-words.
Short, Simple, Strong, Smooth.

Finally, check for accuracy of content, spelling, grammar, and style.

10. Proofread

This is your last chance to make sure it's perfect.

Index

Bibliography

The Creative Brain, Ned Herrmann, Ned Herrman Group
The Whole Brain Business Book, Ned Herrmann, McGraw-Hill
Business Writing and Communication, Kenneth W Davis, McGraw-Hill
Influence: The Psychology of Persuasion, Robert B Cialdini, Collins
Business Writing for Results, Jane K Cleland, McGraw-Hill
Flow, Mihaly Csikszentmihalyi, Harper Perennial
Rules of Thumb for Business Writers, Wienbroer, Hughes, and Silverman, McGraw-Hill
The Artist's Way, Julia Cameron, Tarcher

Acknowledgments

The author would like to acknowledge the work of John Boyle, John Borzi, and Paul Taylor at 6 Degrees. This book is based on workshop material they developed. The author gratefully thanks them for their help in putting this material together. Thanks are also due to Kieran Ots, Glen MacNab, and Simon Cave for their fantastic work on designing the CD-ROM that accompanies this book.